CHILDREN COURAGEOUS
and
Their Families

CHILDREN COURAGEOUS
and
Their Families

Frederick Roberts, M.D.

CHILDREN COURAGEOUS
and Their Families

Copyright © 2003
by
Dr. Frederick Roberts

All Rights Reserved

No part of this book may be reproduced
in any manner without written
permission of the publisher.

ISBN 0-925168-93-9

Cover design by John Mahaffy

Library of Congress Cataloging-in-Publication Data

In Progress

North Country Books, Inc.
311 Turner Street
Utica, New York 13501

Dedication

*Dedicated to the magnificent patients
and their families whose stories
are told in this book.
They have given a new meaning
to the term COURAGE.*

Contents

Foreword

Shortly after I began work in Syracuse, a community pediatrician named Fred Roberts came by the office to introduce himself. I was immediately impressed. Here, I quickly realized, was a practitioner who combined the wisdom of decades of experience with the perspective of continuing to maintain an active, busy practice. My new colleagues on our full-time faculty reinforced my first impression by telling me of the esteem in which Fred was held by both the academic and practicing community. As I came to know Fred, I imagined that his career must have encompassed a multitude of stories.

How right I was. Fred recently came to me and, with his characteristic humility and self-effacement, asked if I would read a book he was working on. Having no idea what to expect, I jumped at the chance. To my delight, Fred had distilled many of the stories I had imagined he had experienced into a unique narrative.

Fred's book provides us with a fascinating look into pediatrics over the past few decades. On the surface, much has changed; on another level, however, much remains the same. We may now know the gene which causes cystic fibrosis and have much more effective therapies. At some point, however, most patients with this disease still succumb to its effects; would that they could all do so like "Timmy"—at home with the comforting presence of a Fred Roberts. We may have more sophisticated ways of delivering insulin and monitoring its effectiveness in children with diabetes, but the problems of children like "Savannah" who neglect their care remain.

There is so much more to Fred's book, however, than a demonstration of the march of medical progress. The world has plenty of books extolling the advances of medicine and the heroic figures driving them. The focus here, however, is on the *real* heroes in pediatric medicine—children and their families. Serious illness and death are always tragic, but when they occur to a child it seems like a perverse reversal of nature's order. Those of us who care for children never cease to be amazed at the strength and equanimity that our patients and their parents seem to find in the face of what we see as overwhelming pathos. These beautiful stories capture that amazement like nothing I have ever read.

As Fred finishes his distinguished career as a pediatrician, Syracuse is building its first children's hospital. How appropriate, and generous, that this wonderful man is dedicating the proceeds of his work of love to this project. I am sure that these children, their families, and Fred's many friends and colleagues, are grateful and proud.

—Thomas R. Welch, MD
Professor and Chair
Department of Pediatrics
Upstate Medical University
Syracuse, New York

CHAPTER 1

⤚⋐⤙

Max and Frank

The emergency room was busy as usual, when I came on duty. My shift ran from 8 a.m. to 8 p.m. and then there would be twelve hours to recuperate. Nothing different this time. Usual number of fractures; mostly broken wrists in seven- or eight-year-olds who had fallen off their bikes or from a tree. There was a drunk or two who needed our attention as well as a frightened girl with an ectopic pregnancy.

The nurse asked me to see an elderly man who had just been brought in by ambulance. He was a pedestrian who had been hit by a car at a busy downtown intersection. The admitting sheet told it all. A witness said he had crossed against the light and the driver couldn't stop in time.

The old man was moaning softly and holding a blood-soaked bandage against his head. His long white hair was disheveled and covered much of his face. He was lying quietly on the gurney while the nurse attached the blood pressure cuff to his arm. He had been immobilized at the accident scene as a precautionary measure and it was necessary to proceed cautiously in assessing the extent of his injuries.

I was startled when I approached the injured patient. He was my grandfather: a tough, courageous, octogenarian who had defied traffic rules for the second time in a year. This time he ended up in the emergency room, bloodied and bruised.

His daily routine since his retirement had been repetitious. Ever since my grandmother's death he arose early, made his breakfast (always had cooked oatmeal, fruit juice and Postum). A quick tidying up of the flat; then the shaving ritual. I remembered it well. He would make up a rich lather in the shaving mug and with the straight razor he had just stropped, would finish his task quickly. Then he would dab the after-shave lotion (it was always Aqua Velva) over his face. The final touch in this daily routine intrigued me the most. I often watched this

1

performance and was entranced as he trimmed his mustache. Little, delicate snips until both sides were exactly even.

Then he would go to his writing desk. It was a roll-top desk with drawers on each side and pigeonholes for letters and writing accessories. He would draft letters to his children and grandchildren who were scattered all over the country. They were long, handwritten messages, filled with flowery phrases but heartfelt. He would reach for his Merriam-Webster dictionary for spelling checks or alternate words. The next step was to prepare packages that were directed to his children. This was a time-consuming chore. The wrapping and secure tying consumed the better part of an hour.

The journey to the post office was a cherished ritual. He'd have his briefcase held firmly in one hand and his walking stick in the other. The walking stick was made of oak. It had a good heft to it. He'd had it for years. It was a gift from his youngest son and was hand carved with my grandfather's initials on the side. He had told me that he didn't need the cane to help him walk, but as a reminder to anyone who might try to steal his briefcase that he was armed and ready to protect himself. The post office was exactly 3.2 miles from his home. I remembered that he made that trip two or three times a week, no matter how foul the weather was.

Now he was in my emergency room. I stepped back briefly and watched him. He continued to moan and moved restlessly on the stretcher. When I drew closer, he opened his eyes and let out a loud distressed cry and fell asleep. Another victim of pedestrian carelessness. I remembered what he had said after his first accident: "They have to look out for me because I have the right of way. The pedestrian has the right of way." We had warned him that all motorists didn't agree with that rule.

Poor old man. I was so proud of that self-educated immigrant. He had a love for language. He spent hours in the library reading Shakespeare, first in a Yiddish version and then in English. When he came to this country from Latvia, he taught in a religious school and in the summer months he became a peddler. He walked dozens of miles every day with a pack on his back, selling soap and perfumes and pocket combs and earrings to the farmers and their wives.

They made fun of his accent and bargained with him over his wares. He'd return home exhausted, with blisters on his feet and only a few dollars in his pocket. But he always had a story to tell. I'd listen to his adventures and wonder if my life would ever be as exciting.

And now my heroic grandfather lay injured in the emergency room. His injuries were serious. He had a fractured vertebra and multiple bruises. The scalp laceration needed suturing and he was hard to arouse. He stirred a little as we injected the local anesthetic and irrigated the wound. I wasn't sure that he realized that I was there, helping in his case.

He was taken to a two-bed room in the Orthopedic ward and I remained in the emergency department, accepting other patients and dealing with their problems.

Near the end of my stint, I called home and spoke to my wife. She had news that worried me. Her bag of waters had broken and she was having irregular contractions. Our first baby wasn't due for another eight weeks and her obstetrician wanted her admitted immediately.

My brother drove her to the hospital and she was whisked up to the Labor and Delivery Unit. I hurried to her bedside, squeezed her hand and consoled her as best I could. As the pains came more frequently, I said that babies do well these days even though they are premature.

Her delivery was rapid. Our son gave us our first taste of parental anxiety when he was hard to resuscitate. He was a wizened little newborn. His color was a terrible greyish blue and his cry was feeble. They placed an oxygen mask on his face, showed him to my wife and then hurried him to the premature nursery.

My wife, Ann, was crying. "Is he all right? Is he going to be all right? Oh, my God, please help us!" My tears at that moment were not tears of happiness.

Every day I shuttled between Max's room and the intensive care nursery. My grandfather was not doing well. He was on a special orthopedic bed and was immobile. He needed to be bathed, fed, and assisted with the care of his bodily functions. I tried to break through the curtain of darkness that shut off contact; he was not with us but somewhere in the past.

Then I would meet Ann and we would visit our son. There were rows of incubators in the nursery. He was connected to an IV line in his arm. He wasn't able to feed as yet, other than by a feeding tube and the staff was unwilling to let us hold him or even touch him. Our baby was in a mechanical womb and we'd have to wait for a later delivery before we'd know that he was really ours.

My years of training had instilled a sense of compassion towards my patients. I learned to listen closely to their histories and tried to respond to their varied needs as best I could. But it was different being a patient yourself or having a loved one in the hospital. There was a fear that grew to gargantuan proportions with each setback that my dad, Max, or our son, Frank, suffered. It was ironic. I was supposed to be a healer and I could do nothing for my grandfather's broken body or my son's fight to live.

The baby rallied . . . or so we thought . . . by the end of the first week, the IV was removed and he was out of the incubator. Ann was permitted to take him in her arms and offer him a bottle. Our baby was doing his part in the fight to survive. He worked hard to swallow the few ounces of formula but seemed exhausted at the end of the feeding and dozed off the minute he was put back in his bed.

We called the intensive care nursery each night for a report. Usually the nurse would tell us that he had gained an ounce or so and he had behaved well. When I called the nursery one evening, I asked how the Roberts baby was doing.

There was a chilling silence and then an unfamiliar voice at the other end said, "Baby Boy Roberts? There's no baby by that name on my list." In shock, I asked to talk to the head nurse. What could have happened? Why weren't we called?

An embarrassed supervisor said apologetically, "Oh, doctor, I'm so sorry. We wanted to surprise you. Your little fellow was doing so well, we transferred him to the regular nursery. I'd meant to call you, but one of the preemies crashed and we've been busy taking care of him."

It wasn't long before we were able to take our son home. I was impressed, not by my knowledge but by my ignorance about the newborn. I knew a great deal about the textbook management of disease, but the ordinary things that concern parents had escaped me; and Ann and I had to learn together.

The other member of my family, Max, did not rally. I buttonholed his orthopedist outside of his room while he was making rounds. Dr. Xavier was very kind. He told the group of nurses, students and house staff that they should continue without him.

We went over to the doctors' staff room on the Orthopedic floor. We poured out two cups of very bitter coffee and selected some chocolate chip cookies and started our discussion. He answered some of the questions about my grandfather's progress.

He refused to offer a prognosis. He said to me, "He's pretty old. You know that. And he's had a serious injury. I've heard that he's tough and resilient, but there's a lot against him. It's a big burden for a man his age. There are a lot of obstacles."

"Of course," I said. "But you don't know my grandfather. The things he's been through in his life would have done away most of us. Somehow he was even able to outrace Malach Hamavet."

"Who?" asked the doctor.

I smiled. "Malach Hamavet, that's the Angel of Death. He's out there, waiting to pounce on his next victim."

"Oh. That's a superstition from the old country, I suppose."

"Yes, of course." Then I added, "It seems to be true in his case, though. He told me about the time he was in the army. He was seventeen years old and his unit was on maneuvers in Russia. They marched to some Godforsaken place, slept in tents, had no heat, no facilities for bathing. They nearly froze to death. On top of that, they were short of rations and half of his company came down with dysentery.

"He figured he'd had enough, he told me. So he left most of his gear in his tent and walked to freedom. He had nothing to eat or drink for two days. Finally he came to a small town that hated the government and the army, and after a few days they found some clothes for him. He burned his army uniform. They wished him good luck and bid him goodbye.

"He left those bitter memories behind and somehow eluded the authorities and found his way to America."

"But you told me that he was seventeen years old then," said Dr. Xavier. "Now he's an old, broken man, lying helpless in bed."

"You're right. But this is Max. He's different. You'll see."

Several days after my discussion with his doctor, Max opened his eyes and noticed a nurse at his bedside. She was a heavyset woman with streaks of grey in her hair and a relaxed manner. She wasn't as businesslike as some but had a warmth that put her patients at ease right away.

"What am I doing here?" he asked. "How come I'm all harnessed up like this? Why do you have these side rails on?"

"It's about time you came to. Your grandson has been very concerned about you. He's been sick with worry. He comes to see you twice a day. He sits beside your bed and talks to you, but nobody's home. You don't answer and so he goes back to work."

"I've been that bad, huh? I don't remember a thing."

"You had a bad accident. Your were hit by a car on Salina Street." She straightened out his pillows and raised the head of the bed. "It's a whole week that you've been here. We weren't sure you'd make it."

When I stopped by one night, after my emergency shift was over, his nurse gave me the good news. She had him all cleaned up. He had his glasses and his teeth in place. He looked like my grandpa . . . not like a homeless person.

I waited as long as I could before telling him that his great-grand-child had arrived prematurely. The details were spared, of course . . . just that when a baby comes early, there are a few problems to resolve.

The circle was complete. We now had four generations, although two representatives were on shaky ground.

Max was full of cheer. He repeated over and over that the two of them would be great buddies and he'd fill the baby full of stories of the past—just the way he had done with me.

Max said confidentially, "This baby. You've named him Frank, after your father. That's a wise choice. He'll be a fighter just like your dad." Then he went on and spun his dream of the days ahead. He'd wheel the baby's carriage over to the park near his house. He'd guard his great-grandson and the two of them would get stronger every day—everything would be wonderful again. With this fanciful dream in his mind, he fell asleep buoyed by the prospects of the future joy.

That was the last happy time Max and I had together; watching him chuckle and feel so comforted that he had this new companion.

Shortly after that, as so often happens with the bedridden elderly, he developed pneumonia. Now he was in an oxygen tent, with antibiotics dripping into his veins. I watched the rapid up-and-down movement of his chest and knew that he would never leave the hospital.

I kept thinking that it was a struggle to live. I had watched my newborn son in the newborn nursery, and now Max's struggle to die. He couldn't beat that lung infection. He was looking skyward, hooked up to wires that sensed his heartbeat and his breathing efforts.

My last memory of him was a bittersweet one. I was dismayed that there was no one who was able to trim his mustache. He wouldn't be ready to walk to a heavenly post office, looking like that. There would be no more excursions, no bold street crossings. They wouldn't have to watch out for him, after all.

My training period was finally over. I had learned some lessons that prepared me for a career in Pediatrics. Max and Frank had taught me that the lives of my patients were filled with battles—some we won, some we lost.

CHAPTER 2

The Atwater Family

There are all kinds of valor. The marine in a steaming jungle; the cop facing an inner-city gang; the fireman rescuing an elderly woman and her cat; the boxer, overmatched, trying to last ten rounds; the wife fending off blows from her alcoholic husband. Many more instances of bravery can be cited but my heroes were none of the above. They don't rate headlines nor do they receive medals for their acts of bravery. They are found in the daily battles of everyday people. Children and parents who have been caught in the major wars of daily survival, who often are unnoticed but who have earned my admiration. I'd like to tell their stories.

A physician is a privileged person. He or she enters the patient's life in a variety of ways. Sometimes during a crisis; at others, it is a chance encounter that may lead to surprising results. One such family was introduced to me nearly twenty-five years ago.

The essence of the Atwater family's struggle cannot be told with clinical data only. The various terms we use in medicine cannot describe despair, fear, triumph or love. Some diagnoses carry with them a sentence of death or disability and then, as doctors, we retreat and carry out our therapy but we are observers, not suffers. When we deliver a solemn prognosis, we are uncomfortable but our lives are not altered by the news. This is the Atwater family's story, as told to me, in their own words.

The saga began on April 20, 1975. Craig Kimberly Atwater, Jr., was born seven weeks prematurely, weighing only three pounds, ten ounces, in the college town of Potsdam, New York. His dad was twenty-one and I, Valerie Atwater, was nineteen, very young parents who were overjoyed with the thought of a newborn baby to call our own. My husband was in his senior year at Clarkson University, soon to graduate with honors with a degree in Industrial Distribution. It was a rough start for us, as neither of us had a steady job and were struggling to make ends meet. However, in spite of the challenges, we could think of nothing that could make our life more complete than to have a child with whom to share our lives. The labor was rapid and delivery uncomplicated, aside from the suddenness of it all. I delivered Craig after about one hour of hard labor, by natural childbirth.

He was a fighter from the first cry. I can't remember his Apgar scores, probably because I didn't even know what an Apgar score was at the time, but he was breathing on his own and was put in a rather primitive isolette. The rural hospital did their best to maintain him; however, the next day he was transferred to Crouse Hospital Neonatal Intensive Care Unit with a diagnosis of hyaline membrane disease, thirty-three-week gestation, difficulty breathing—but an otherwise healthy infant. He would have been flown by medical jet, but the plane had left with another more critical patient. They whisked him away the next day in a fully staffed ambulance. My feelings were profound, not only from the separation of a mother from her newborn baby, but that perhaps I would not see him again for this lifetime, should his condition worsen. The next few days would determine how his future would unfold, and there was nothing to do but wait, hope and pray. They gave him a fifty/fifty chance of survival, but those odds never dampened our faith. I kissed him goodbye and prayed very hard.

He did very well under the care of the specialists in the unit despite his low birth weight, immature feeding pattern and underdeveloped respiratory system.

I went to Syracuse to live with my parents, while Craig remained in Potsdam to finish his studies. I spent my days at the hospital trying to learn how to be a new mother and keep up the faith that he would survive. Each day the doctor would make rounds and stop by to fill me in on the baby's progress, always displaying a kind and positive attitude, guiding us along a road that we never dreamed we'd be traveling. After each conversation with me, she would then take time out from her busy schedule to call my husband long distance, to reassure him, as well, of the progress of our son.

Craig came home to us weighing four and a half pounds. He had developed apnea while he was feeding. He went through many tests to determine whether or not he also had sleep apnea, but they were all negative. As time passed so did all of the problems of prematurity; and he started to become a "baby" again. At this time, we had the services of Dr. Roberts and his group to care for him, and his childhood was uneventful for the most part. After his early difficult times, he was a picture of health until his illness which began in 1998.

Our second son, Chad Thomas Atwater, was born on November 20, 1976; full term and weighing six pounds, one ounce. It was a beautiful, calm pregnancy, resulting in a serene child. Perfect in every way. He slept through the night after two weeks. Chad had numerous childhood illnesses but overall was very healthy. He was a quiet, loving child who made it very easy to be a parent.

The two boys grew up to be very close—where one was, the other wasn't far behind. And what a joy to have them, although we were exhausted at the end of the day.

In 1978, we discovered that a new addition to our family would be forthcoming. We weren't prepared for this so soon, but accepted it as yet another chance to add to our growing family.

The pregnancy was unremarkable except for an episode of bleeding at two months. I was put on complete bed rest, and within two weeks the bleeding had subsided. I woke up one morning with severe dizziness and localized abdominal pain, which didn't feel like labor pains to me. About ten minutes after I reported this to my doctor, I started to hemorrhage at home. We didn't wait for an ambulance. Craig carried me down three flights of stairs, into the car, and sped to the hospital.

Aaron's birth was very complicated. I had a complete placental abruption, which completely severed the baby's blood supply. I lost almost three units of blood, and his heartbeat was undetectable upon arrival at the hospital. They delivered him quickly by Cesarean section. I can remember, before they put me under anesthesia, I was crying and pleading for someone to tell me if my baby was alive. There were so many doctors and nurses in the room, and so much chaos, that no one seemed to be able to answer me. The anesthesiologist came over and took my hand and said, "You are a very sick young lady, and we are concerned that you are losing a lot of blood. We need to take care of you. As for the baby, we will do everything we can to save him."

With these words, I was a little more at peace, knowing that there was a chance for the baby and that we were both in good hands.

When I awoke, I asked if the baby had lived and if I was going to die. It was my greatest fear that I would die and not be able to take care of my children, especially the one who had the greatest fight for his life.

The events that followed Aaron's birth were the most trying times we had endured so far. He was in the hospital for nine days, most of those days being a series of tragic downslides. The doctor predicted that his disabilities would be in the moderate to severe range, and said that many children with severe impairments such as his, do not survive past age five, mostly due to respiratory failure. He was up front, yet he was compassionate and helpful, giving us several avenues to pursue regarding community resources to help us with his care. He left me with his phone number, in case I ever needed anything. We were blessed with caring, dedicated medical professionals to guide us through, for we surely felt we were entering a world of uncertainty.

It wasn't hard to love Aaron. He was a child who had endured many obstacles, from constant respiratory infections and seizures, to numerous hospitalizations and surgeries. His constant medical needs made it difficult sometimes to divide our time among the three children, but Craig and Chad seemed to adjust very well. They were both always very helpful and loving to him. Craig grew very close to Aaron as he grew older, and was eager to learn how to care for him and even learn to feed him at an early age. He always stood up for Aaron if people would stare or verbally pity him in his presence. He would say, "He's my brother and he does lots of things. We even have a teacher come to our house to teach him how to hold things in his hands and look at toys." Oftentimes, I would see him near Aaron singing his favorite song to him, "You Are My Sunshine." It wasn't until twenty-two years later that the true meaning of that song was revealed to us.

It seemed as though it would be difficult for Craig and Chad to grow up with a brother who was so ill at times that they wondered what would happen next. Yet they always stood by him during those times and rode out the storms, as we all did. We all admired his courage, perseverance and, most of all, his ability to face each day of his life with a smile. His happiness was maintained through his family, and we would have life no other way for him. It wasn't easy, but we were committed to do everything that we could to care for him at home and give him the best life that he could possibly have.

Twenty-two years have passed and he is still with us. Aaron has become the epitome of a hero in his own right and, through his innocence, has proved to be the most powerful force of life for his family. His courage has taught us many lessons of the meaning of life, love, and what it means to be part of a family.

May 18, 1997, was one of the happiest days of our lives as parents. Craig graduated with honors from Clarkson University with a Bachelor of Science in Interdisciplinary Engineering and Management, at the same university and the same course of study as his father.

In July of 1997, Craig started his first position as a manufacturing engineer for a large company in Ft. Wayne, Indiana. He moved out to Indiana all alone, with no friends or family nearby, and I knew that this was a very difficult adjustment for him. He started out working very hard, often putting in long hours; and when he visited us at Christmas time, he looked visibly tired to me. He was still working a lot of hours and, when we spoke on the phone toward the middle of February, he again complained of fatigue. He said that there were many days he would work from 7 a.m. to 6 or 7 p.m., come home and go straight to bed and sleep right through the until the next day.

He also casually remarked about a "rash" that was on his ankles and asked me what I thought it might be. Of course, from all of the years of medical education with Aaron, they thought surely that I had my degree in medicine and they should expect me to come up with a diagnosis.

When he described the rash as tiny pinpoint red dots that almost looked like a bruise, I panicked to myself. I told him he needed to make an appointment as soon as possible to get it checked out. He assured me that he felt fine, other than being tired and the rash. I told him that it could be something serious, such as leukemia. He thought that was absurd and said, "There you go again, thinking you know everything about medicine!" But he agreed to make the appointment.

The first think that came to my mind when I heard of his symptoms was a friend of mine when I was six years old. She was diagnosed with leukemia. I remember playing with her in the yard one day, and the next week, when I had my tonsils removed, she was in the next room, dying. I thought she was having her tonsils out also, and my mother gently told me that she had "cancer of the blood" and was probably going to go to heaven soon. I stood outside of her window the day that I went home and waved to her, and never saw her again.

It took Craig about a week or more to get established with a doctor, to get an appointment; but he reassured me that he felt fine. On the day he went to the doctor, I waited to hear from him, until late in the evening. At about 9 p.m. we received a call from the emergency room doctor at Parkview Hospital in Ft. Wayne, telling us that our son was gravely ill. His platelet count was 2,000—the normal being 150,000 to 200,000—and he was very weak. They had run a battery of tests, and the doctor thought that he either had aplastic anemia or leukemia. I asked to speak to him, and he could barely talk, he was so exhausted. He told me that he was scared, that he was by himself in the room, and that he was cold. He was crying. If I could have jumped over fifty states at that moment to be there, I surely would have. His father packed his suitcase and flew into the car, to start up to the hospital. Chad, Aaron and I would follow by airplane the next morning.

The next four days were a whirlwind that we would never forget. The staff at the hospital was quick to diagnose his severe aplastic anemia and arrange for him to be transported to a transplant center. We were told so much information that we could hardly absorb any of it, and walked around dazed most of the time. We did, however, comprehend the seriousness of it all. Unless one of the other siblings was a perfect or close-to-perfect match for a bone marrow transplant, Craig was going to die; and the chance of one of them having a 6/6 antigen match was about twenty-five percent.

Chad accompanied him aboard the medical jet bound for Strong Memorial Hospital in Rochester, New York: We followed with Aaron in the car. Craig was admitted to the Hematology/Oncology floor there, which was a very hectic place to be. It seemed that every week someone died there, and it was always very intense. We came to know a team of doctors and nurses from the Transplant Unit, who would become our family, of sorts; who would literally take our son's fragile life into their hands. One of the nurses, in particular, was instrumental in his recovery. She was close in age to him and had the gift of compassion in her job, yet was tough on him at times, somewhat like a coach, to keep him in shape for the challenges that he would face. It takes a very special individual to be a transplant nurse, who is so directly involved on a daily basis with a patient whose chances of survival are usually quite slim. Seeing so many patients die, after spending months nurturing them, has to take its toll after a short while; yet their dedication to the profession and their genuine human compassion allows them to pick themselves back up and offer the same hope and faith to the next patient.

Cases of aplastic anemia are very rare, in general. We were told that Strong Memorial may see one per year. The immediate plans were to keep him stabilized and free from infections, and do HLA testing on Chad and Aaron. Preliminary tests came back revealing that neither sibling was a match, so they decided to start him on ATG, a horse serum, to see if this course might bring up his counts. They explained that it could be a very lethal drug and could cause a severe systemic allergic reaction. We felt we had no choice but to try this while waiting for an unrelated donor.

Several days later, after results of the HLA testing came back for a final doctor's approval, he noticed that the technician had relayed the wrong message regarding compatibility. After he carefully reviewed the results, he quickly called down to the floor to alert us that Aaron was, in fact, a perfect 6/6 match. We almost collapsed with joy. I had felt in my heart all along that it would be him. To this day, the original lab reports are framed and hanging in Aaron's room, and it is still unbelievable to me to see the numbers, listed exactly the same. Craig finally had his chance of surviving. We didn't realize, then, the obstacles he would have to face to continue his fight.

Looking back, there were subtle signs of Craig's deteriorating condition. He started to require more frequent transfusions to maintain his platelet count, and began to acquire infections that were resistant to many of the antibiotics. His father traveled back to Indiana to tie up loose ends and, at Craig's request, to bring his belongings and his prized possession, his Honda, back to New York. Chad had to fly back to North Carolina to register for his classes at UNCC.

The evening that Chad left, Craig was doing poorly. They were trying to fight off an infection with a different course of antibiotics. They said their goodbyes, as brothers do, in a very matter-of-fact "I'll see you soon" manner. When Chad went outside the door, he said to me, "I wanted to say more to him but I couldn't." I think he thought that he wouldn't get the chance to tell him the things that were in his heart. Throughout the ordeal Chad was the pillar of strength for us all. He maintained a positive, straightforward attitude. He would sometimes get angry at all of the emotional upheaval that we, as parents, displayed. His philosophy was to give his brother nothing but a positive atmosphere, and forge ahead with faith, regardless of how dismal things seemed. And the best part of it was that he truly believed all along that his faith would prevail and his brother would recover. Both my husband and I said that, if it weren't for Chad steering us straight, we never could have survived this emotionally. His part in this was equally as important as Aaron's, in that just by his presence we were all comforted.

Craig's condition worsened. He had developed a high fever, swelling of his extremities and was having difficulty putting words together. They monitored him closely, and waited until morning to reassess his condition. The following morning they called me at the Ronald McDonald House to tell me to hurry to the hospital, that my son was in respiratory distress. It was thought that he had an anaphylactic reaction to the ATG. When I arrived at his side, he was crying and told me that he had been gasping for air and couldn't breathe. His words were, "I was to the point where no matter what I did, I couldn't catch my breath and it was getting harder and harder to breathe. My stomach hurt so badly from breathing so heavily that I felt like the next breath was going to be the last time I could do it . . . and then, all of a sudden, I 'felt' a comforting voice, filling my head, telling me to relax and breathe slowly. It was like a moment of realization that if I just focused on my rosary and relaxed and breathed slowly, then I would be okay again."

The rosary that he was referring to was a purple rosary that my mother had given him before she passed away, and he swore that he thought it was her presence with him, reassuring him and that took him through the ordeal. After several hours it subsided and it seemed the worst was over.

Toward the end of that evening, he continued to run a high fever and still was having difficulty staying on track with his thoughts. By the next day, his oxygen saturations were dangerously low, registering in the 87 to 90 range. He was rushed to the ICU, where they determined that he had dilated cardiomyopathy due to both the allergic reaction and the systemic infection. The doctor told us that his ejection fraction was about twenty percent at best, and if the medications didn't take hold soon that he wouldn't survive. He was very weak and they were nearly ready to put him on a respirator. He also had periods of hallucinating one minute and being very outspoken about his bone marrow transplant the next. He was determined that the doctor hold a meeting with him to start planning when they would do the transplant and start making plans to get Aaron ready for this. This was devastating to us because we had to try to explain to him how sick he was, all the while knowing that the transplant, quite likely, wouldn't occur. We were in agreement with the doctors to keep his attitude positive, however small his chances were, and not tell him that the transplant wasn't an option at this time.

My husband and I were overcome with grief. We tried hard to make sense of it all. Why now, after so long and so many miracles that were given to us, would he not survive? The only explanation we could think of was that perhaps God looked down upon this child of ours and had plans for him in a better place. If that was the answer, we had to accept it. We prayed harder than ever.

The next day brought good news—the medicines had started to work and his heart was functioning better. After three days, he was transferred down to the Bone Marrow Transplant Unit. It took him about a week to recover and return to his normal mental status as well. He was transferred back down to Hematology for another two weeks, until preparations were made for the transplant. He then was readmitted to the Bone Marrow Unit.

Many considerations had to be made for Aaron to become the donor. The doctors had to determine whether he would be a suitable donor in view of his past and present health status. They reviewed the added risks for Aaron's fragile condition and, after a careful workup and cytogenetic testing, they contacted his pediatrician, who gave the go-ahead.

Craig went through chemotherapy and total nodal radiation for preconditioning for the transplant. He did well through this, compared to most patients, but still had many side effects. He got to the point where he was so weak that his dad had to help him into the shower one day. Afterwards, he sat on the bed in his father's arms and sobbed, "Why am I not getting better? What is happening to me?" That was the first and only time he broke down. It had taken its toll on him, and we felt helpless and feeble, unable to do something to ease his mental exhaustion.

On April 28, 1998, Aaron A. Atwater donated his healthy bone marrow to his brother, Craig K. Atwater. We were filled with renewed hope that Aaron's cells would give Craig a new and healthy life.

For Aaron, this was a piece of cake—or at least, in his own way, he tried to tell us that! He woke up from the anesthesia after the bone marrow extraction, wide-eyed and smiling. He had two little incisions on his back, which by the next day had nearly healed. He appeared to be completely free of any pain when he was moved around. It was as if nothing out of the ordinary had occurred.

Fourteen days later, Craig's counts appeared, and then flourished each day after that. We felt that we were truly blessed and began to breathe a sigh of relief, but we were cautioned that there was a risk of graft-versus-host disease and also of increased risk of contracting infections, and how dangerous that could be. He was, by far, not out of the woods.

He came home at the end of May, but had to return to the hospital for an appendectomy in June. We all had stayed with him for a total of three months; I stayed an additional two months while he recovered to the point where he was comfortable getting back to life on his own.

I remember a conversation that we had had before the transplant and after he had recovered from the ordeal in the ICU. He was in a fairly peaceful frame of mind and was talking about the transplant, and how he just wanted to "go ahead NOW and have it over with, so he could get the hell out of the hospital." As I listened, my heart was sinking as I thought to myself, "What if he has another complication or the transplant isn't successful? What if the graft-versus-host reaction or an infection takes his life?" I reassured him that we were all anxious yet hopeful that the transplant would cure him. And I quietly added, "Are you aware of the risks that are also involved, the ones we talked about?"

He turned to face me, and looked me straight in the eyes and said. "I want you to know that I am not afraid to die. I know all about the risks, even though I don't like to discuss them. If I have the choice of living the rest of my life in and out of the hospital instead of having the life that I've always known, or taking the risk of the transplant along with the risk of dying during or after the transplant, I will have the transplant."

At the moment of those spoken words, I respected the man my child had become, and sat speechless.

The bravery, determination, faith and enduring spirit that Craig showed, continues in his life today. He never takes anything for granted. He is a free spirit, full of life, and is now living his dreams to the fullest. He hasn't forgotten what it is like to go through something as profound as a life-threatening illness that forever changes one's life. And he has told me on many occasions that, as horrible as it was to experience, he will never allow himself to forget it, for that would take away the importance of the lessons in life that it had taught him.

As for Aaron, he has achieved the honor of being the reason that his brother is alive today. How ironic that this innocent, fragile child, with what so many would call "severe limitations," would rise above them all to the apex of fortitude and heroism.

CHAPTER 3

∿

In Search of a Troll

Lucy was a longed-for baby girl. Angela's pregnancy was uneventful and Lucy weighed in at five pounds and she was eighteen inches long. She was a bundle of pleasure to her parents with dark coloring, a shock of coal black hair and long eyelashes. Everyone saw a little bit of each parent in the baby. It seemed like a dream come true.

Lucy did not grow as she should. She wouldn't nurse despite her mother's patient efforts and when in desperation, after a series of formula changes were rejected, they turned to my office for advice.

When I saw her in the office, the baby was lost in the blankets. Her luminescent dark eyes were the only signs of humanness. There was a coarsening of her features that I had not noted when she was in the nursery. It was not uncommon for newborns, particularly for those who were early, to have a fine mantle of hair, known as lanugo, over their arms and back, but Lucy's was dense and black.

Her weight was a scant five pounds. Not an ounce had been gained in the two weeks since she was discharged from the nursery. When her mother lifted her from the scale, Lucy stiffened and began to scream.

She had a shrill, unending cry and when Angela tried to console her, did not calm down. She resembled a miniature doll but was neither cute nor cuddly. She arched her back when she was handled and her head bobbled loosely when she was lifted. She wouldn't focus on objects and her parents were certain that some terrible misfortune lay ahead.

After a worrisome passage of time, the crying stopped and she fell asleep. Her color was ashen grey with blueness of her lips and nailbeds. Angela carried her over to an examining table and Lucy curled up into the fetal position once more.

When I examined the baby, I was disturbed to find that her abdomen was distended and that she had a loud heart murmur. She was in heart failure and needed an immediate referral to a cardiologist.

The weeks following her first office visit were spent with multiple tests and medication to stabilize her failing circulation in preparation for cardiac surgery. The family was shaken by this crisis. There were no facilities at the time in our region for the type of surgical care she needed. It meant a trip to a large center at great emotional and financial cost. They would need to be prepared for a risky operation without assurance of success.

The prospect of a long recovery in a distant city with no comfortable support system was a hurdle of major dimensions. I could offer the family no alternative. It was either a repair of the cardiac deficit or the sure loss of Lucy.

The hospital personnel were kind and understanding. They answered all questions in detail, and were with the baby around the clock. All of the hopes for a magical improvement, though, were illusory. The surgeons were brilliant but Lucy's cardiac abnormality was complex, and only partial correction was possible. She remained in the critical care unit for several weeks before she was upgraded from serious to fair.

While Lucy was at the medical center, the family learned that my fears were justified. She had a rare genetic disorder that had many unfortunate manifestations. The heart problem was only a part, albeit a major part of the cluster of abnormalities that made up the syndrome. They were informed of the hearing, skeletal and visual defects that sometimes were companion pieces of the disorder. There was no way to resolve the many handicaps that would occur as she grew older. She might be rescued from one facet of the disease but another burden was always in the wings waiting to test Lucy's survival.

We were able to give Lucy's delay a name. Doctors classify a group of findings as a syndrome. This cold word codifies the miscellaneous features so that the outcome can be predicted. By definition a syndrome is a "pattern of symptoms in a disease or the like; a number of characteristic symptoms occurring together." In her case it was called Morquio's disease, a mucopolysaccharidosis.

Placing a label on a baby's symptoms does not alter the outcome, nor does it deal with the family's agonies or soften the blow to their hopes for their child.

When they brought her home, Lucy was more than six months old. Most of her life had been spent in a hospital setting. It was time to establish a routine for home care. There didn't seem to be enough hours of the day to feed her, bathe her, give her the many medications she needed, play with her, and try to establish a measure of normalcy to her babyhood. There was no reason, the family felt, to wallow in self-pity. They had prayed that she would survive the surgery and now they were presented with her care for the rest of her life, no matter how long or short it might be.

One tiny baby with so many needs. It was a learning experience for the young couple. There was not a Dr. Spock book to serve as a guide, instead it was discover-as-you-go type of baby management. There were trips to my office, or at times, my trips to their home, each time hoping for some sign of progress.

Lucy was a fighter. She managed somehow to overcome everything that stood in her way. She added weight slowly and at two years was the size of a ten-month-old. The features of her rare syndrome were more evident. She was a cruel caricature of a young child. Strangers would turn away, afraid if they stared it would disturb her mother.

By degrees she learned to walk, not minding the bumps and falls along the way. Her babble grew into phrases and sentences strung together in melodic cadences. She had an endearing way about her. Her giggle and smile made everyone want to cuddle her and forget what lay ahead. That road was laced with potholes and she found them all.

Lucy was one of those children who qualified for an early intervention program. Her parents joined a support group and regularly attended conferences dealing with children with special needs. Fortunately, there were enough enlightened caregivers in the community who realized that all children deserved to have their lives enriched. In many parts of the world, the children like Lucy would be warehoused and ostracized like lepers.

They found a small nursery school that fit Lucy's needs. The director's son had Down syndrome and Lucy was accepted without hesitation. The two of them were different from their playmates but the program found room for all of them.

In this climate, Lucy blossomed. She had friends and did not feel isolated. Despite her handicap, her level of development inched along in tiny increments.

It was not the same when she had to leave the shelter of the nursery school. She was enrolled in a preschool program and there her differences set her apart from the other children.

Angela and Charley were very much involved in Lucy's education. They took turns reading to her. The stories that filled Lucy's ears were the usual fairy tales; some Dr. Seuss and A. A. Milne's *Winnie the Pooh* as well as those that Angela made up for her daughter.

The bedroom would be darkened with only a small night light on. The two of them would sit propped up in bed with the world shut out for a short time. Lucy had a favorite story. She wanted to hear it every night and if Angela changed a word or two, she'd have to start over from the beginning.

There are many romantic figures in literature. Who hasn't thrilled to the ugly duckling's transformation to a lovely swan? How many versions of "Beauty and the Beast" have led young people to fantasize that they can be like the fictional characters?

Of course, it was a cruel hoax. In reality, Lucy was the same misshapen child who looked more like a gargoyle than Snow White.

Angela was not her usual self when she brought Lucy to see me. Her patience was exhausted and she seemed defeated. I waited for a few minutes, played a few games with Lucy who smiled at my silliness and waited for her mother to prepare her for her annual exam.

Angela touched a handkerchief to her eyes and tried to compose herself. My nurse walked to the scales with Lucy and came back with a printout of her height and weight. She had gained only a pound and a half in a year and was the size of a child one-half her age.

There was nothing new of concern during the exam. Lucy needed some booster shots for kindergarten and there was an obligatory urinalysis and an eye and hearing exam. The nurse arranged for these test and Angela and I had a chance to talk.

"I can handle almost anything, doctor," she said. "You know that Lucy is my life. She's got so much to deal with but I can't get her to smile the way she does with you. She must realize that she's not like other children but we can't shelter her forever. Do you think it's right for her to start kindergarten this fall? Charley and I are going crazy trying to figure out what's best for her."

There was no way that I could give her the perfect answer. For years we had been mainstreaming children with all kinds of problems through the public school system. Educators and parents alike gave the program high marks but way down inside of Angela's mind there was doubt that Lucy was ready to face her peers. Would she be crushed by the experience or would she be embraced by the other children and treated as an equal?

My wife and I had planned a vacation in Europe for many years. Something always came up and we put away the travel brochures sadly—for some time in the future. One of our friends told us of the magnificence of the Scandinavian countries and our interest was rekindled. We flew to Oslo, took a train to Bergen and boarded a cruise ship that hugged the shore lines of Norway en route to the Arctic Circle. We saw the rugged coast with its mountains and wondrous fjords. It was a trip that we would never forget.

There were hours when we would sit in an area of the ship where we could view the beauty of Norway through floor-to-ceiling windows. For a short time we were at peace with the world and I never wanted to leave the splendor of that country and return to the frantic pace of life as I knew it, yet sometimes my thoughts returned to the problems that I had left behind during this two-week escape from reality.

The image of little Lucy popped into my mind. I wondered what could I bring her from this foreign country that might brighten her day.

Our ship stopped at many ports and we toured the gift shops looking for souvenirs for family and friends. I gathered all sorts of little tokens for my family and friends from the Land of the Midnight Sun. When we returned to the ship, they were packed away in our luggage. I added a coloring book about reindeer and Laplanders from the ship's store as well as a doll that was popular in Norwegian folklore.

When we returned home, I found that I had been invited to Lucy's birthday party. She was celebrating her seventh birthday. Her family made each of her birthdays into elaborate events.

Her father carried Lucy into the dining room. He placed her on her booster seat at the head of the table. A sad little princess. The relentless march of her disease had coarsened her features more than ever. You could tell that she suffered more than physical pain because the smile that had softened her appearance was no longer evident. Instead there was a perpetual frown that crisscrossed her forehead and her eyes were red and puffy from the tears that fell too often.

Charley had hired a clown and his antics amused her cousins, aunts and uncles and brought a flicker of a smile to her face. There were games and songs, the customary ones at children's parties. Then the hot dogs and hamburgers and French fries and soft drinks were served. Next came the cake. A great layered cake with a topping several inches high, pierced with seven tall candles. Her father lit the candles, motioned to Lucy and she obliged with three feeble breaths.

The stage was set for the gift giving. The packages were opened one by one and the presents were placed on the table beside Lucy. Wind-up toys, necklaces, furry animals, picture books, puzzles and the like cluttered the table. When each one was presented, Lucy responded with a "Thank you very much."

Her Aunt Josie bent over and kissed Lucy and put a life-sized doll near her niece. It had blonde hair, an organdy dress, a real pearl necklace and a china face with flawless features and deep blue eyes.

She also received a set of Barbie and Ken dolls, beautiful ones from Spain and Greece, as well as a Native American doll; all dressed in their authentic costumes.

Lucy offered her thanks in a quiet voice. Then she suddenly leaned forward and swept the collection off the table. She turned to her father and begged to be taken to her room.

Everyone was silent. Angela tiptoed back from Lucy's bedroom. She looked to her family and friends and said apologetically, "You must excuse her. She hasn't been feeling well lately, but she insisted on having her party. I don't know what happened just now."

The guests waited several minutes, chatting with one another and then left.

I asked Angela if I could have a word with Lucy. She consented and I carried my Norwegian cargo with me to Lucy's room. She was in bed, her Dad was at her side. He offered me a chair and left the room.

"I'm glad you invited me to your birthday party," I said. "Got you some things when I was on vacation this summer. Nothing very fancy. But I thought you might like them. The kids in Norway do."

She seemed to be interested. I gave her the little gifts and then with a flourish reached into my bag and pulled out a large, ugly, big-nosed, hairy Troll.

"You can name him anything you want," I said. "I'm sure you'll come up with something special."

Lucy's eyes brightened. She blew her nose and then picked up the Troll.

"Oh, Doctor," she cried out. She hugged the hideous-looking creature. "I love him. He'll be the first one to understand how I feel. He's even homelier than I am so I'm going to take good care of him. He needs somebody who cares, he really does."

CHAPTER 4

ॐ

Altered States

Accidents, homicides, suicides. These are the big three that cause serious injury or death in childhood and adolescence. It was chance that resulted in the events that altered the lives of several of my patients.

There were three sisters under my care. Their father had died and the family managed on the mother's income. Fortunately they didn't need much medical attention, just routine health exams and the assortment of immunizations and sports evaluations that society dictated. The oldest daughter, Tina, a petite thing, was the perpetual student who had a book in her hand most of the time. She was destined for something great. Her school, church, family and friends kept her occupied for the most part and although she wasn't as outgoing as her sisters, she found time for the lighter side of life. There were a few boyfriends and a lot of parties in her senior year of high school.

It didn't surprise anyone when Tina was named valedictorian of her class. Her speech at commencement was full of idealism and she pledged to use the award for outstanding achievement towards a career in medicine. She asked me if she could shadow me in my office during the summer for a little advance taste of a doctor's daily life. I was flattered and gladly granted her request. Later I learned that I was not the only one impressed by Tina's ability. Her church had assured her that they would underwrite the expense of medical school if her grades in college were of the same level of excellence.

Her sisters cheered during the awards ceremony but their interests weren't the same as Tina's. They counted up the years of study Tina would need to reach her goal and felt that they would look for something that called for less sacrifice.

I shared the family's pride. Tina could do anything she put her mind to. It was a pleasure to fill out the college physical exam and know that she was launched.

On the way home from her senior ball everything changed. Tina was seated behind her date on his motorcycle when he hit a pothole in the road. She was not wearing a helmet; he was. Her head injury was massive and when the ambulance hurried her to the hospital, she was rushed to the operating room immediately. Sylvia, her mother, called me and asked me to sit with her and be her information messenger during the long wait for news. I shuttled back and forth, gathered whatever progress report I could get.

How hard it is to be the bearer of bad news. Her brain had been so badly damaged that some portions were beyond saving. The operative procedure took hours and the prayer was for life. Full recovery was impossible.

Tina was comatose for days. Sylvia looked for some sign of hope but there was none. It was more than six weeks before she was ready for discharge. She was to be sent to a rehabilitation center first and her mother would be taught how to provide basic care. After that she would need help in gaining daily living skills. My role was limited. I had been her pediatrician and cheerleader. But this wasn't a simple case of asthma or pneumonia; something I could treat. It was an effort to return her to kindergarten capabilities. Her speech was limited; she was emotionally labile with tears one minute and uncontrollable laughter the next. The accident had found her judgment center and destroyed it. Tina needed help in walking and the simple tasks of dressing herself or combing her hair were yet to be regained.

Sylvia spent hours every day at the rehabilitation center. She consoled herself with the knowledge that Tina was alive and, maybe with hard work and progress, she could function again as part of the family.

I visited Tina every couple of weeks. There wasn't much difference that I could see from one visit to the next, but the only substitute for everyone's hard work was surrender. Sylvia accepted little gains with gratitude. It was boring, repetitious work exercising weak muscles and trying to regain lost skills. Tina was no longer a calm, studious girl but a young woman with a short attention span and miles to go before she could return home.

There was one reason for optimism. It could be termed serendipity but another one of my patients had traveled a similar route fifteen years earlier.

I recalled the day a plump, grey-haired woman carried her granddaughter into my examining room. She smiled as the nurse unwrapped the pink blanket from the baby and watched as she was weighed and measured. She was told that I would be in shortly and she was asked to fill out a questionnaire while she was waiting.

She put the baby in her infant seat and looked over the list of questions. She started to fill in the details of Saundra's brief life, let out a deep sigh and looked over at her granddaughter. It wasn't a pretty story. To her it was unthinkable that any infant would start life with such a disadvantage.

Saundra's head drooped slightly but she sucked noisily on her pacifier and seemed to be at peace. A lot different from the time when she would whimper and start to twitch; first with little facial jerks and then violent convulsive movements. The ordeal was repeated over and over, sometimes fifteen or twenty times a day.

Mrs. G. began to write about Saundra's mother's pregnancy. Her son and daughter-in-law, Patty, were planning to be married when she finished high school. The pregnancy was an inconvenience but was accepted at first as a temporary detour in their plans. After the baby came, Patty intended to enroll in a beauty school, obtain her license and help Harold support the family.

The dream didn't materialize as she hoped it would. The awful nausea in the early part of pregnancy drained her enthusiasm for childbearing. She cried uncontrollably when the doctor told her that it was too late for an abortion. She stayed shut up in her room most of the day and filled the ashtray to overflowing with her cigarettes. Harold didn't know how to handle her dark moods and remained in the background, hoping that Patty's feelings would change when the baby arrived.

Mrs. G. filled out the questionnaire as best she could. She wrote about Patty's massive weight gain and swollen ankles. She noted that the obstetrician had told her son that the delivery went smoothly and that everything seemed all right with her new grandchild. Mother and son stood in front of the nursery window staring at the baby, telling each other that Saundra was the prettiest infant in the nursery. She was pink and white with delicate, doll-like features and deep dimples in each cheek. Mrs. G. could hardly wait for the chance to cuddle and rock Saundra and watch the wonder of her growth in the years ahead.

Patty remained withdrawn and refused to hold the baby and asked the nurses to keep her in the nursery for her feedings. Harold and his mother couldn't understand her strange behavior but the doctor reassured them that many women had postpartum depression and it should clear when she left the hospital and was back in familiar surroundings.

Mrs. G. hadn't finished when I came into the exam room. She handed me the record and she lifted the baby out of the infant seat and placed her on the table.

"Please go on," I said. "Tell me what happened after Saundra was discharged from the nursery. I didn't take care of her, you know, until she was admitted to the Pediatric floor two weeks ago. I know about that, of course."

Mrs. G. began to cry. "My son and I kept waiting for Patty to take charge of the baby. You know, like her OB man said she probably would be her old self again in a short time. But she just moped around the house, telling Harold to feed the baby, change her diapers, bathe her and all that. She said she wasn't ready yet and went to the bedroom, turned the radio on and shut the door.

"I didn't know what to do," she continued. "Harold had to go to work and so I took over for awhile. Not that I minded. Saundra was a precious baby. I finally called Patty's doctor and he phoned in a prescription for some kind of tranquilizer and again said that these things take time but that Patty would be all right."

She stroked Saundra's cheek and went on. "The doctor was the authority, not me or Harold. We did what we were told to do, filled the prescription and after a few days Patty seemed a little brighter. Maybe I'd forgotten how let down you sometimes feel after you give birth. After all, it's been a long time since I had a baby.

"Well, Doctor, I had some business to attend to downtown and left Patty with the baby." She reached for another tissue and dried her tears. "I wasn't gone for more than an hour. When I walked in the house it was quiet. The bedroom door was closed and when I opened the door I nearly went crazy. Patty was lying on the bed, smoking a cigarette and reading a magazine and Saundra was in her bassinet." Mrs. G. began to sob again.

"There was blood on the sheet and the baby wasn't moving. There was big lump on the side of her temple and her face was all swollen." Again Mrs. G. paused, cleared her throat and started once more. "Patty just stayed on the bed . . . didn't say a word. I screamed, picked up the baby and ran to the other room. I called the ambulance and they rushed her to the hospital."

At that point I took over. "Your son called me that evening and asked me to see Saundra. The neurosurgeon had worked on her for three or four hours and she was in the recovery room. She had what we call a subdural hematoma. Her skull had been fractured and the surgeon had to operate so that the large collection of blood could be released from the surface of her brain.

"You knew all about that part, I realize. Your grandchild needed a lot of help but they did a great job just to save her. Now I guess we have to take over and see what we can do."

Mrs. G. undressed the baby and I saw what we had to face. There still was some swelling and discoloration of one side of her head. Her arm and leg on the opposite side of her body were limp and useless. She was able to cry and suck on that pacifier though. The other and most disturbing feature was the muscle weakness, the paralysis of her eye muscles.

It was going to be a tall order for Mrs. G. to take care of this wounded baby. Patty had been admitted to the Psychiatric Hospital as the result of her attack on her infant daughter. It was to be the first time that I had been asked to care for a victim of abuse by a parent.

Unfortunately, Saundra was merely the first of many. There would be cases of the so-called shaken baby syndrome; of murder by suffocation; of burns and deliberate starvation. All varieties of innocent children suffering at the hands of a tortured parent, either strung out on drugs or responding to some demon within their minds.

This time, though, the strength of Mrs. G. allowed a different outcome from most. Her daughter-in-law remained an inpatient at the Psychiatric Hospital for most of Saundra's childhood. And her son, Harold, was a willing but ineffectual player in his daughter's life.

What seemed like a hopeless task, gradually was less gloomy. I'd read many times about some dedicated person nursing a wounded bird back to health and I'd admired their patience and tender caregiving. But this was a battered child with damage to her brain as well as to her body. The fixing of everything that went wrong consumed most of Mrs. G.'s days. She would not consider hiring an aide to handle the time-consuming task of feeding her grandchild. The baby was not able to suck well enough at first to maintain growth. She was cradled in her grandmother's arms and the formula was dispensed by dropper in small amounts. It took an hour by the clock to finish a six-ounce bottle. We calculated the number of feedings per day, multiplied them by the calories per ounce and arrived at the figure needed for growth. Mrs. G. spent six hours each day dripping nourishment into the baby. Six hours spent in the simple chore of feeding but the hidden bonus was the close contact with someone who cared for a helpless baby, who rocked her and sang to her and encased her with a protective love.

Anyone who has been involved in rehabilitation knows that results don't come quickly. Fortunately, there was an excellent support system in our community with a team of physiotherapists and occupational therapists who guided Mrs. G. through the monotonous exercises that began as soon as Saundra left the hospital. They fell in love with the little blonde child and her grandmother and knew that Saundra's future was dependent on their skills. There is a point in most cases where further progress is not possible. Each time Saundra seemed to reach that stage, Mrs. G. would beg them to try a little longer and to everyone's delight another milestone would be reached.

Speech and language development was another story. Saundra's brain damage presented a challenge to the neurologist and the speech teachers. At first there was a question as to her cognitive level. Her perpetual smile with or without stimulation made it hard to test her accurately. Brain-evoked response testing was necessary to discover whether she could hear. Then to figure out whether sounds had meaning for this child was another task. In the beginning Mrs. G. and Saundra learned to sign together. But in time single words were mouthed by Saundra and bit by bit a useful vocabulary was built.

In spite of all the joint efforts of the many therapists, Saundra was not able to be made whole. Her left arm and leg were spastic and of limited use. Her eye muscle paralysis was not able to be corrected completely. The glasses that she hated to wear helped a lot and made her look quite wise.

The remaking of a little girl was far enough along so that she was able to be enrolled in a special kindergarten class. I asked her grandmother to bring me Saundra's picture so that I could post it in a place of honor on my bulletin board. There have been many times throughout the years that I got a lift just looking at that photo. She was wearing a blue dress with squiggly white lines across the front and across her sleeves. Her shoes were polished to a bright shine that day and although they didn't show in the photograph, I know that her outfit had been planned for weeks ahead and they should be mentioned. The smile that illuminated her face, to me, was even more wonderful than Mona Lisa's famous enigmatic smile.

I have often taken the photo down and read the words on the back:

"First school picture, Sandy Lee G. Age 7."

It didn't matter that she was two years older than the other kinder-gartners. She was there, waiting to be part of the class.

Saundra struggled to keep up with her class, but she managed to finish elementary school (special education) and I snapped another picture of her in cap and gown. Then she dropped out of sight. She was accepted in a new training program for handicapped people and was lost to me. She was now a grown young woman and was way past the age for a children's physician's care.

It was a wonderful surprise when I paid my every-other-week visit to Tina at the rehabilitation center. Tina was in a wheelchair and was being taken to the swimming pool for some aquatic exercises. When she spotted me she waved and motioned that I should come to her side. She enjoyed the swimming program and it seemed to be helping her recover some motor strength. Her morale was better than it had been since the accident and there was a reason for optimism.

Her escort locked the brakes on Tina's wheelchair and came around to say hello. She looked very professional in her aide's uniform. I was given a big, unprofessional kiss from Saundra, recently hired and, by some quirk of fate, assigned to Tina.

∽

CHAPTER 5

A Noble Experiment

She was sitting in my waiting room again. This time it was not with a baby for me to examine but she just wanted to talk. I hadn't seen her in six or seven years and my curiosity was aroused. She was pretty far along in her pregnancy and our meeting had to be about her past problems with Rh disease.

Her opening remarks confirmed my suspicions. This time we might not be able to help her. She was in her seventh month and her obstetrician was afraid that she might lose the baby. This was her eighth pregnancy; she had had one stillborn and two normal births when the problems began. The last three pregnancies had resulted in babies who were jaundiced, anemic and needed exchange transfusions right after birth. It was touch and go for the last one and we were lucky that she pulled through and had no damage from the blood group incompatibility.

That was seven years ago and now here she was again at thirty-nine trying to have another child. She didn't pull any punches. "I've been reading about a new treatment for Rh disease," she began. "My OB man tells me that I'll never carry this baby to term. All of my tests are bad—even worse than the last time if that's possible. He wondered if you had any experience with this treatment, he says it's worked for some mothers like me."

I had been involved in the management of a great many babies with Rh disease as part of my general pediatric practice. Her three babies had been treated in the conventional way and had survived. But they had been followed through the last weeks of pregnancy and were transfused right after birth. This baby would not be able to be carried far enough to be handled in a similar fashion. An intrauterine transfusion was a desperate way to extend the pregnancy. No one in our medical community had experience in the procedure but we felt that we could recruit the necessary specialists and tide the baby through the vital extra weeks in the uterus.

She waited for my answer. I wasn't going to deny the enormous risks involved both for her and the fetus. She knew from her last pregnancies how close we had been to losing the babies and there had been openness in discussing the prognosis then.

"I think we can get a team together that can try to do an intrauterine transfusion. You should know that there's a high risk of failure in the best of hands. We have to thread a long needle through your abdomen. We have to make sure it's placed properly and then we have to inject about two ounces of blood into your unborn baby. If everything goes well, you will be able to keep the baby alive for about three or four weeks and then we can treat him or her right after delivery."

I looked at her. She had been nodding as if she understood the whole operation. "There are no guarantees that we can help you. It's sort of a science-fiction way of treating an unborn baby."

She got to her feet. "Doesn't seem to me that we can do anything else. The baby is still moving inside of me . . . I can feel her kick me every so often . . . it's going to be a girl again . . . I think that I would go crazy if nothing was tried and the baby died."

Then she added, "Think about it. I don't know where else to turn. I know you'll do your best and I trust you completely."

This was a little like climbing Mt. Everest but I wouldn't have a guide and my colleagues would be flying blind right along with me.

We talked for another fifteen minutes or so. She was such a brave woman to consider such an experimental treatment. She was taking all of the chances. There was an obstetrical risk that she had to face and the baby might never make it, intrauterine infusion or not.

There were other considerations, of course. She had five other children, a husband and a big farmhouse to manage. She had considered all the options and had asked me to help.

All of the consent forms were signed. Both parents were ready for this medical adventure. Our team was worried that their hopes were too high despite our caution that the odds were not in their favor.

She was the calmest person in the operating room. We shook hands before I scrubbed for my part of the procedure. Mine, not hers, were the ones that were cold and moist.

Fortunately there were no glitches. Everything went as well as if we had done hundreds of these procedures. The baby received the injection of blood and her heart rate remained strong. There was no hint that our pioneer intrauterine infusion had failed.

She was cheerful when the time came for her to be induced. The baby had continued to grow in her womb and was big enough now so that we could deal with the major problem of Rh incompatibility and not prematurity as well. The baby was born alive but needed several blood exchange transfusions before our worries were over.

More than thirty years have passed and Rh disease is no longer a common problem. Women are now given RhoGAM, a substance that suppresses the development of antibodies that can lead to fetal damage or death. It has been effective and we are called upon infrequently to treat infants with such extreme measures.

The woman who was willing to submit to a new, risky procedure might have been forgotten by me if I hadn't come across a newspaper article in my files. The novelty of an intrauterine transfusion had attracted one of the science columnists of our local paper and the mother and baby were celebrities for a few days. There was a photo of the two of them; she was holding her daughter as her medal of honor, her award for valor.

On impulse, I looked up her phone number and dialed it. She was surprised that I remembered her and her children. Everybody was fine, she said, and we made a date for a reunion later in the month.

This time I saw a silver-haired, very attractive, non-pregnant woman. She introduced me to her youngest daughter, our lucky experiment. Her daughter was holding her own youngster. There were hugs all around—not very professional, but understandable.

It was a flashback moment when the years reversed and in my mind's eye, I saw her walk into my consultation room and ask for my cooperation.

CHAPTER 6

❧

Savannah

She was angry. Not just at me but towards everyone who touched her life. Juvenile diabetes carried a threat to her survival but she was reckless nonetheless. What was the sense of diet, exercise and three shots of insulin every day? It wasn't going to cure her disease. She would have to take those shots for the rest of her days. All that jive about being like everybody else didn't fool her. That's the same bunch of lies they told her when her first attack of asthma landed her in the emergency room. Use your puffer when you have tightness in your chest, don't smoke or be near anyone who's smoking, and get rid of your cat right away.

Who could live like that? Especially when you were expected to give up your pet. The ball of fur that crawled on your lap and made your stinking world a little better just by being there.

She still had those coughing spells even when she followed some of the doctor's directions. The ones when your chest feels tight and you wonder whether you'll ever be whole again.

Her nightmare never stopped. She was sick and tired of hearing her mother fight with whatever guy she brought home. Their drinking and pot-smoking made it impossible for her to get any rest. They didn't want her around. She was in the way—as disposable as the empty six-pack.

It was not much better at her great-grandmother's house. There was that smell that she noticed around old people. And her great-grandmother certainly was old and full of complaints. Savannah was sure that the arthritis wasn't so bad that the house couldn't be a lot neater. Dirty dishes in the sink, wastebaskets filled to overflowing and an eighty-year-old black lady still in her night clothes in mid-afternoon. But this woman was the only one who cared for her without reservation.

Her whole world was full of defeat. How could she go to school with those spoiled college-bound kids and not feel resentful? They bunched together and talked about proms and trips to Europe while she dreamed of a fix that would make things livable for a few hours.

When she'd come to the office in the middle of a diabetic mishap she would be unreachable. She refused to keep a log of her blood sugar levels and couldn't be convinced that she would feel better if she followed the program we'd outlined for her. I was certain that she had a strong death wish but hadn't quite reached the time when she'd take the steps that would release her from her misery.

As she sat on the examining table she mumbled curses in my direction. I knew instinctively that she didn't hate me but she wouldn't open up when I asked her what bothered her or if she had seen her counselor at school. She covered up every window that looked into her life. "Shit, shit, shit, doctor," she blurted out. "My goddamn stomach hurts and I can't hold anything down. Not even a piece of toast. It's been like this since yesterday."

It could be that her blood sugar had skyrocketed and she might be in need of another trip to the hospital. "How did you get here?" I asked. "Who came with you?"

"My great-grandmother," she muttered. "She's in the waiting room."

We ran the usual tests, checked her urine and blood and to no one's surprise the results confirmed that her diabetes was out of balance. We had added another test at the last minute and told her that we were checking for drugs and pregnancy as well.

She was too sick to deny that either might be positive and she asked if her great-grandmother could keep her company while we waited for the lab results and for the insulin to kick in.

The old woman had a calming effect on Savannah. She was the one who never passed judgment on anyone. She told me that she had ten children and fifteen grandchildren. Most of them had turned out all right, she said, but her granddaughter, Savannah's mother, had messed up big time. "Of course I love her," she had said, "but she's been a worry from the day she was born. Quit school; didn't look for work and chased around with a wild crowd." She turned towards Savannah.

"This poor child. My granddaughter had her when she was fifteen. Didn't stop her from running with her friends. Let her mother take care of Savannah. Never gave a damn about her. They stayed with me for a time. It wasn't easy but we managed."

She looked over towards Savannah. "Feeling better, honey? As soon as the doctor says you can go, I'll call a Medicaid cab and take you to my place."

Savannah was too tired to offer an objection. We had started an IV and were rehydrating her, hoping that she would stabilize enough so she wouldn't need hospitalization again.

Her great-grandmother went on, "My daughter, Bessie, loved Savannah and tried to bring her up the right way. Lurinda, that's Savannah's mom—certainly is a mixed-up family, isn't it, Doctor? She moved in with her boyfriend and never bothered about the baby."

I let her know that I had been Savannah's pediatrician from the start and I remembered when Bessie was diagnosed with breast cancer. "That's when you took over," I said.

"Yes. Bessie tried, right up to the end. She died when Savannah was in kindergarten. Lurinda tried to take care of Savannah but she couldn't change her lifestyle and she'd ship her back to me."

Some of the strength from that old woman must have found a spot in Savannah's life. When the pregnancy test came back positive, Savannah began to cry. "What the hell can I do now? I can't take care of me, a baby—Oh, no. That son of a bitch wouldn't use a rubber!"

She stared at me and then sat up and held her arms out to Billie. They hugged each other for a few moments. Savannah pulled the IV out of her arm and said in a surprisingly calm voice, "I didn't think I'd get pregnant. Stupid, isn't it? Half of the girls in my class have babies. I can handle it if they can." The defiant look returned and she said, "I'm not going to kill this kid. It's a lousy world but maybe this one can have a chance."

And then she gave me a rare smile. "Hey, Doc, will you help me? I promise to change . . . at least I'm gonna try. I never said that before, did I?"

It's so easy to make pledges. In Savannah's case she would need to make pacts with a great many devils.

Billie helped her great-granddaughter to her feet. I looked at her. There was no defeat in her eyes. She had seen several generations crumble and Savannah was her last chance for family survival.

Billie put on her floppy hat, reached for the prescriptions I'd made out for Savannah. She looked at me through the Coca-Cola prescription glasses, gave me a thumbs-up sign and left the office.

Juvenile diabetes and pregnancy are a difficult combination. I didn't know if Savannah would have the staying power needed in the long months ahead.

Whether it was Billie's prayers, Savannah's new-found cooperation or her obstetrician's skills, I'll never know. Her baby was early but needed only an extra few days in the nursery before she could be sent home. She was a normal, beautiful infant.

There was no way of knowing how long before Savannah would go before she reverted to her old habits. Maybe I had the answer when Savannah and the baby came for the first office visit.

Savannah had a jauntiness I'd never noticed before and the baby looked like a little princess. She had someone to love now and there was a sense that her maternal instincts would not disappear overnight.

Perhaps it was just a happy beginning but we'd have to settle for that now.

CHAPTER 7

❦

Ronaldo

How do you say goodbye? I watched as the friends and family passed by the open casket. A little boy was at peace at last. He was dressed in a dark suit with a white shirt and bow tie and shiny shoes, hair neatly combed, asleep. There was a bulletin board on a table with dozens of pictures showing different stages of his brief life. None featured a child with a toy in hand, nor with a ball or stuffed animal. Each was taken indoors with Ronaldo lying passively in his crib or sitting propped up in his chair. You could see a suggestion of a smile in some of the photos, but in others there was a frown or a look of pain. And in every one you could see the nasal prongs that carried oxygen to his lungs—that he needed from birth until his last breath. I looked over at the boy in final repose and realized that that part of the life support was missing. Gone too was the gastrostomy tube for his daily feedings and the nebulizer for the every-four-hour inhalation therapy. No horde of antibiotics or cortisone drugs could be seen.

The family was dry-eyed and when I offered my condolences they were accepted numbly. I had witnessed so many desperate scenes in the emergency room when the ambulance had rushed him in for crisis management. I had watched as his mother held his hand as the rescue medicines were administered and he was shuttled to a hospital bed for days of treatment until his breathing was easier and he could return home again.

Ronaldo was a premature birth who weighed less than a small stewing chicken. There was a three-month stay in the newborn intensive care unit before the neonatologists turned him over to me for further care. They had been triumphant in defying nature and were able to declare their version of victory. He was sent home with an apnea monitor; a tracheotomy tube in place; cylinders of oxygen for constant use. His mother had been briefed on a list of vitamin drops, iron medication, special high-calorie formula, daily number of cc's of prednisone to be given. He was oxygen dependent, steroid dependent and, most of all, mother dependent. He had bronchopulmonary dysplasia as well as apnea of prematurity, retinopathy of prematurity and failure to thrive.

Ronaldo was released to the loving care of his mother. She was to provide all of the duties of the nursing shifts at the hospital as well as managing her four other children and running a busy household. The tiny apartment was filled with the machinery that kept Ronaldo alive. This full-time task was accepted without complaint, at least to me. Every time I saw Ronaldo he was immaculately dressed and his mother knew every detail of his medical routine.

There were at least a dozen times that he was admitted for respiratory distress. He seemed to be suffering and I could almost see a pleading in his behavior to escape. There was no joy in his life. On one occasion when his respirations were in the seventies and he was cold and dusky, I asked his mother if she would want to have a Do Not Resuscitate order in his chart . . . that when it appeared hopeless, should we go on with our attempts to reverse his downward slide.

She looked at her little boy, then at me and shook her head. "No, Doctor, no. As long as he is on this planet, I want you to do everything you can to keep him alive." There was nothing more I could say. She knew the prognosis was hopeless. She knew that there would be more spells when it was sure that he could not survive but somehow he would.

There was no miracle. Her strength and love were not enough. She treasured every day and when the end came we all bid Ronaldo goodbye and knew that, for her, there were no regrets.

CHAPTER 8

❧

The Learning Curve

The assistant principal sat next to me at a testimonial dinner for one of our school nurses. We were there to honor a woman who had made a lasting impact on everyone around her. There were ripples of laughter intermingled with solemn side conversations. It was time to say goodbye to her with toasts and gifts and wish her well in her retirement years. There were so many things we could say to her. We could thank her for the way she calmed the frightened kindergartner with the skinned knee, or the asthmatic girl pulling for air, or showing the new diabetic how he could treat himself. No matter how impressive these abilities were, the audience was celebrating something else. She had learned the rare art of nursing the hidden wounds as expertly as those that were visible.

"She told me those twenty-seven years raced by," my companion said. "Most of the time she was at our school. She tolerated all of the changes and adjusted to everything. Everything except children who couldn't smile and didn't know how to play."

They would be serving the first course soon and most of the guests headed toward their seats. "We never talked about the new kind of kids," I said. "We were both trained in the old ways. As a matter of fact, we worked at the same hospital before she joined the school system. We used to talk about how formal nurses were. Their uniforms were starched, their caps sparkling, their manner professional at all times."

"It all changed some time ago. These used to be neighborhood schools. Most of the children walked to class; nobody was bused and the families were a lot alike. All Italian or mostly so in one section of town; Jewish or Polish in another. They formed their own little islands."

The conversation went on. "It all got scrambled. People moved out to the suburbs and the new families couldn't speak English and clung to their customs and had little or no trust in the schools or the teachers."

The dinner had started and we drifted into the banquet hall. We heard the speeches and applauded when she received her award. I knew that she would be lost without her place among the children. She would hope that life in a motor home was an escape from all the troubles at school. But the freedom wouldn't last. Her thoughts would return to the years of nursing and the grip it had on her life. Sunsets and towering mountains would never be replacements for the daily adventures with her patients. The open road and campfires and flat tires couldn't compare to the pleasure she had found in her work.

The assistant principal continued to reminisce. She told me of the time she sent a seven-year-old to see her. His teacher thought he must be sick. The whole class was taking a standardized test and he just sat and stared at his paper. He hadn't answered any of the questions and when the teacher asked him why he was so pokey, he began to cry.

"What was the trouble? Was he sick? A fever?" I asked.

"No," she answered. "Nothing of the kind. He was a bright little boy and he would have done as well as any of the others if he'd tried. But he wasn't interested in the test or school or any of us."

The boy stayed in the nurse's office for more than an hour. She didn't say a word to him but waited for him to ask to leave or at least have his mother come and get him. In the meantime, other children visited her for minor complaints. Their problems were managed quickly and they returned to class. His sobs had stopped at last and he looked at our nurse and he blurted out the reason for his strange behavior.

"There wasn't anything under my pillow, Mrs. W." He pointed to a space between his lower teeth. "They got loose and I put them right where I was supposed to. When I looked, nothing was there. Wasn't yesterday and wasn't this morning either. She forgot all about me."

She nodded but didn't speak. His wailing grew fainter and he jammed his thumb into his mouth and found some comfort.

"Sometimes people forget things, Jimmy," she confided. "I know how you must feel. Everybody forgot my birthday one year and I hated my whole family for a while. We had just moved into a new house and there were millions of things that had to be done. They didn't mean to hurt me . . . it just happened."

Then she added, "The tooth fairy must have gotten the wrong address or something. You didn't move, did you? The way I did?"

"No, Ma'am," he said. "We're in the same place. She just didn't remember. That's all."

The crying started again. In deep, heaving waves. Mrs. W. stepped back. She walked over to a cabinet near her desk and returned to the boy's side. She handed him a box and whispered, "I keep these for the times somebody doesn't remember birthdays or teeth the tooth fairy forgot."

He took the package, opened it up and found a large, Slinky toy inside. He wiped the tears from his eyes, played with the gift and noticed there was another treasure buried at the bottom of the box. He placed the Slinky carefully on the desk and lifted the bright, red, musical yo-yo out where there was room to put it through its paces.

Then he stopped, placed his rewards back in the box. He went over to Mrs. W., planted a wet kiss on her cheek and ran back to class.

This story resonated. I remembered a little girl from Bosnia and how Mrs. W. and I shared some incidents about that child's misery.

As a school physician during the years of international upheaval, I had examined many children who had found a safe haven in U.S. cities. They were innocent victims of unspeakable terrorism in their native lands. Revolutions and counterrevolutions uprooted millions from their homes. Our community accepted the humanitarian challenge and tried to provide a chance for a new life in our midst. That meant a place to live, clothing, food and employment if possible, education for the children and basic health care.

The children had to cope with new customs and a foreign language and were overwhelmed. I tried to put myself in their position and recalled my experiences during World War II when we had shore leave in a strange land. There was no way I could understand the signs, the language of those foreign countries. And I was only a casual visitor who went back to my ship and remained with my comrades.

A six-year-old girl from Bosnia was enrolled in a course called ESL, English as a second language. She had mastered a few words and understood simple questions such as, "How old are you? Do you have any brothers or sisters?"

She answered the first one easily, frowned over the second but finally held up two fingers. She was a lovely child with brown hair and deep eyes. There was a long scar on the right side of her face, just below the cheek bone. Her pupils were not equal and when a light was flashed into her eyes, I realized that she had a prosthesis. A bomb fragment had damaged her eye during the ethnic cleansing.

It was a sobering realization that this tiny victim of war carried such a burden.

Several months later the school bus slid on an ice-covered road en route to school. The children were not injured but as a matter of policy had to be examined. Most of them were amused by all the attention they received. Mrs. W. brought the six-year-old Bosnian beauty over to me. The child was sobbing uncontrollably and was holding her left eye. A small swelling was present. Nothing more serious. Her terror was real. What would she do if she lost the sight of that one good eye?

One of the nurses at a senior high school was a close competitor of Mrs. W. She had to deal with problems that were new to the teaching and the health care system. The real threat of violence from scissors, guns and home-made bombs made modern nurses front-line warriors.

One morning when I was doing a mandated school physical for tenth grade students, the nurse was my chaperone as an eighteen-year-old awaited her turn. She was an enormous Afro-American student who was in a special education class. She filled the chair to overflowing and waited expectantly for me to begin.

"Have you missed any school for sickness this year?" I asked. She shook her head, no.

"Have you had any accidents or injuries? You know—stitches or broken bones?" Again, no.

"How many cigarettes do you smoke a day?" A standard trick question.

She didn't fall for it. She glared at me and said, "I don't smoke at all and I don't do drugs or drink no beer."

Somewhat chastened, I started the examination. Her hair was greasy and unkempt. There were no nits or head lice at least. Her eyes were charcoal in color and, except for the annoyed glare she aimed at me, were normal. Her teeth could have benefited from some good oral hygiene and had a few caries. Her face was satiny, round and without acne. She was wearing large, long earrings that hung down almost to her shoulders, almost obscuring a sizable area of deeper skin pigmentation on each side of her neck. I was approaching a sensitive topic and I didn't want to antagonize her again. I looked over at the nurse and then mentioned casually, "When Mrs. C. weighed you today, there was quite a difference from the last time."

"I know," she said.

I went on as carefully as I could. "Three hundred fifty-three pounds it says on your record. That's up from two hundred forty pounds a year and a half ago. That's quite a bit of weight in that time."

She answered quickly, "Yeah, it is. That's because I had my baby. She's a year old now."

"I see. Well, while you were pregnant did you show any sugar? Did the doctor tell you that you had what is called gestational diabetes?"

"Didn't see no doctor at all until I started with pains near the end."

"How come you didn't have a doctor?"

"'Cause I didn't tell anybody I was having a baby. When you're big the way I am, people can't always tell."

"Was your baby all right? You said she is a girl. Did you have her the natural way or did you have a section?"

"Natural."

"How much did she weigh?" I asked. "Eleven pounds, two ounces."

Mrs. C. looked surprised. "We never knew about your little girl," she said. "You didn't miss much school, did you?"

"No, ma'am," she said proudly. "I was back in class in a coupla weeks. My aunt is taking care of Tanika."

I finished the exam. The patient sat in her chair while the nurse and I moved to the side of the room out of earshot from this unbelievably obese girl and talked about my findings. I told her that the darker skin pigmentation on her neck is a marker for insulin-resistant diabetes. The intense skin color is called acanthosis nigricans. Her huge size may be part of that condition as well.

We knew that her future was at risk. She had so many strikes against her. Poverty, learning disability and an inadequate support system. Her aunt was the only relative involved in her life.

Then my nurse took over. She would make this student's health care her responsibility. She'd make sure that there would be a place in the helter-skelter world of today and wouldn't be lost in the maze of HMO's and clinics where there might not be any advocates for the helpless girls who face situations like this.

Acanthosis nigricans—she wouldn't be able to spell the term let alone grasp the significance of the condition. It was yet another obstacle in her life. She had been alone for a long time but I felt that she could muster up enough strength to beat the odds. After all, she had Tanika to bring up.

She got up from her chair and waddled toward the door. She thanked us for being interested in her health.

"Where do I go to get my working papers?" she asked the nurse. "I've got a job three nights a week at the Thrift Shop. It's great workin' there . . . right near where I live and I can get all my baby's clothes for nothin'."

CHAPTER 9

<small>∽</small>

To the Last Breath

Early in my career I became interested in caring for children with cystic fibrosis. It had been identified as a specific disease entity more than sixty years earlier and presented an enormous challenge to the medical profession. There was no cure (nor is there now). We had some primitive forms of therapy and kept searching for better ways of helping our patients with special diets and new and more effective antibiotics as well as techniques for clearing the lungs of its thick tenacious mucus. My interest led me to start a clinic exclusively for children with cystic fibrosis.

We met twice a month in a space in the hospital basement. None of us had any specific training, just the desire to learn more as we went along so that we could improve the quality of life of our patients. Before long our files were filled with the clinical records of many infants, toddlers, school-age children and even a few adolescents. There were no survivors in those early years past the mid-twenties.

Every special clinic dealing with chronic and often incurable diseases grows close to its patients. They are unforgettable. We watch them fight to breathe, to gain weight, to be part of the everyday world and inevitably see them slip away.

I remember one child whose mother had had nine children before her only baby with cystic fibrosis was born. She was a skinny woman, weighing less than eighty pounds for sure. Her daughter was severely involved right from birth. The baby's intestine was blocked by a thick plug of a material called meconium and surgery was needed when she was three days old to clear her lower digestive tract. She failed to thrive from the start and required replacement enzymes and a special formula as well as additional vitamins and iron.

Her early weeks of life were spent in the hospital. Every day, as soon as her other children were off to school, she would arrive at the hospital. She lived several miles away and her only transportation was

48

a bicycle. She would lock her bike at a stand in the parking lot, carry her lunch box with her and sit at her baby's crib side until mid-afternoon and then cycle home to care for the rest of her brood. The same schedule was repeated daily. She could hardly wait for her baby to be well enough so that she could take her home and try to fatten her up. She looked used up herself. We wondered how she could keep going with all those children at home needing her attention and the newest member in such desperate condition. She shrugged her shoulders when the social worker asked if she had any help at home. There wasn't anyone else around. Her mister, she said, took off as soon as he knew that she was pregnant. Then she'd look at the baby again, smile and tell us that she could manage and ask when would her baby be discharged because she'd need to get things ready at home.

Sad though it was to have a baby with cystic fibrosis, the effect on a family was crushing when more than one child had the symptoms that were the hallmark of the disease. We watched two brothers reach college age only to lose their battle a year apart. In another instance three children failed to make it past their twelfth birthday. The oldest child was in the hospital when she died and then her brother went to a research center in Boston but did not show any improvement despite the most advanced technology including a bronchoscopic washout of his thick secretions. He lasted another month in our local hospital.

When the same sequence of pulmonary congestion and heart failure began with Tim, their youngest child, they begged me to care for him at home. They recognized the futility of therapy and did not want the coldness of an institution during the final stages of his life.

One winter night I received the anticipated call from the parents. Timmy had slipped into a coma and they asked if I would be there to share the painful burden of bidding goodbye to the last of their children. I went to the driveway of my home, cleaned the windshield of its accumulated snow. I was the preceptor for Andy, a young medical student who was interested in Pediatrics, and I invited him to join me on this sad home visit. Timmy's parents had met him during one of their crisis calls at the hospital emergency room and would accept him as a witness at life's end.

We drove to their home. It was about ten miles from the center of the city. It overlooked a magnificent valley but was nearly inaccessible during the harsh winters typical for our region. The drifts were towering and the snow plows could not keep up with the heavy snowfall.

We waded through waist-high piles of snow toward the garage door entrance. We hung our overcoats on the hooks inside of the garage, shed our boots and entered the house. Our patient, Timmy, was still alive. He was in his own bed, his favorite toys beside him. It was only a matter of less than an hour before his breathing stopped. I motioned to his parents to step out of the room while I verified that he had, indeed, died.

The scene was so natural that I wondered why it was not the preferred way to have a life end. No loudspeaker bellowing out a Code Alert. No troop of nurses and doctors pushing a crash cart into the room and carrying out the "heroic" measures that could not sustain or restore life.

Andy and I left the room while Timmy's parents wept at his bedside in private. Then I called the funeral director and waited for him to fight his way through the storm. The death certificate was signed and my student and I collected our winter garb, said goodbye to the bereaved parents and headed back to the city.

Andy told me many years later that he never forgot that night. He felt that we had performed a service more meaningful to the parents than a pronouncement of death in a public arena. It was easier for them to let go this way.

Gloria's illness took a different path. She fought the many burdens of her illness just like the others. She longed for every joy of normal living and found an understanding boyfriend when she was sixteen years old. Bruce ignored the coughing spells and the shortness of breath and learned to assist in her care. He even became proficient in the chest-pounding that was part of her daily physiotherapy. He kept track of the multiple medicines she needed and brought hope into her life.

Gloria became pregnant shortly after they were married. Her condition worsened in the early months but she refused to have an abortion. Davey was born at full term. He was a handsome little fellow without any signs of cystic fibrosis. The pregnancy had taken its toll on her and when Davey was less than a year old, she was hospitalized with a collapsed lung. It took two weeks before she was well enough to go home. Bruce and Davey were waiting for her, ready to resume their mutual struggle with her illness.

I made a home visit to check on her progress and discovered that she was a compulsively clean homemaker. Everything was well organized—places for Bruce's things, the baby's, and counters and shelves for her needs.

The nurse and I went into the bedroom with Gloria. She looked tired and frail. There were large bruises from IV entries and her skin had an odd yellowish cast. Her breathing was rapid and shallow and every time she coughed she held her hands against her ribs to lessen the pain. Her lungs were still full of fluid and her heart couldn't pump blood fast enough to provide energy. She was nearing the end and she knew it.

We saw the equipment stationed near her bed and learned that she and Bruce slept in the large double bed inside a mist tent. Davey's crib was within reach and she told us that the hum of her compressor lulled him to sleep.

There were so many similar histories. Most of them had the same ending. Months or years of struggle waiting for the miracle that would liberate them.

One sad story appeared in our local newspaper. It told of Jimmy and is reprinted here in its entirety. Robert Kinsella was Jimmy's principal and he and Jimmy's mother have allowed me to share their memories of the brief life of an unusual boy.

To the Last Breath

Jimmy lived only nine years. From 1959 to 1968. He was a student at Minoa Elementary for just three years.

Almost from birth his mother knew that something was wrong. Jimmy could brighten her life with his smile, but he was unable to move as her other children did when they were his age. He couldn't hold his head up or even move about.

The frequent medical exams, however, always came back normal. Finally Mrs. Gerry D. insisted that the doctor come to their house and see him in his normal environment. After the visit and many tests later the doctor advised his parents, "Your son has a severe case of cystic fibrosis and there is nothing we can do. He will die before his third birthday."

Mrs. D. changed doctors that day. They all loved their new pediatrician, Dr. Frederick Roberts of Syracuse, who now takes care of her three beautiful, healthy grandchildren. Under the guidance of Dr. Roberts, Jimmy passed his third birthday and enjoyed playing with his few friends.

Jimmy carefully chose his friends. He sensed those who would reject him. He could ride a bike if it was on level pavement. He loved to read but his great love was the Chicago Cubs. He knew every player and every year he was certain that his Cubs were going to win the World Series. (Sammy Sosa would have been his idol.)

In the summer of 1966, Mae Ryan, a first grade teacher in Minoa Elementary School, where I was the principal, tutored Jimmy at home in Fremont. In the '60s and early '70s, few handicapped children went to a regular school.

Society at that time felt that it was best that they be taught at home or educated in a special school away from the "normal" child. Out-of-sight, out-of-mind was the philosophy of the day.

Jimmy was a smart, friendly boy who didn't understand why he had to stay home when all the kids in the neighborhood got to go to school. Mae had naturally fallen in love with the trusting little blond-haired boy. She often shared her many stories of Jimmy with me.

She was helping him with some math problems one day when he began asking questions: "Mrs. Ryan, am I as good a student as the kids in your class?" He looked up at her seriously and she answered him honestly.

"You're better than most."

"Do you like teaching me?"

She put her arm around the frail, little body and gave him a hug. "I love teaching you."

Jimmy stared down at his paper and twirled his pencil. Mae waited patiently, wondering what was coming next. Finally, he looked up and asked quietly, "Mrs. Ryan, if I am as good a student as your other children and you love teaching me, why can't I go to your school and be in your class?"

He jumped up excitedly, saying, "I'll be good and work hard! Please! Please! I want to be like other kids and go to a regular school." In his eagerness, his skinny hands gripped her shoulders, but his grip was so weak she barely noticed it.

"I promise, Mrs. Ryan, I won't make you ashamed of me."
When she didn't answer, he turned and ran from the room.

Mae looked down at the paper they'd been working on.
Suddenly she was angry. "Jimmy, come back here," she
shouted. His white face appeared in the doorway. "Jimmy, you
will go to regular school, and you will be in my class."

Suddenly, he was next to her, his thin arms stretched
around her waist, hugging her with all his feeble strength.

I remember vividly when that little yellow bus arrived for
the first time in the fall of 1966. I was Jimmy's principal and I
kept thinking that I had made a big mistake. Maybe he would
be better off in a school where the other children were like him.

The door of the bus opened. Out stepped a blond-haired
little boy. He wore a new green shirt with a wide collar and tan
corduroy pants. With great determination, he moved across the
sidewalk, placing each foot carefully in front of the other. He
was breathing hard and his skinny arms seemed too small for
the metal lunch box and brown paper sack he was clutching. As
he approached, our eyes met.

"I'm Mr. Kinsella, your principal. Welcome to our school,
Jimmy."

Jimmy looked up with a big grin. His smile transformed
the pale, fragile creature into a happy little boy.

"Thank you, Mr. Kinsella," Jimmy said shyly. "Thank you
for letting me come to your big school."

Mae knew that Jimmy's appearance might seem peculiar.
She also knew that his disease was not contagious but because
Jimmy coughed a lot, which is a symptom of CF, she decided
not to tell the class what was wrong and how serious it was.

She also knew a common misconception was that people
might catch the disease from him coughing near them or even
being in the same room. Mae knew it was an inherited disease;
no one catches CF and it can't be given to anyone else. Yet she
knew what she said to the children was critical if they were to
accept Jimmy as just another child, not one with special needs.

Jimmy was quickly accepted by the other children in his
class, especially by Skip Letcher, a popular athletic boy. Skip
adopted Jimmy the very first day of class and they were soon
inseparable.

Both top students, they would hurry to finish their work so they could work together on extra projects. With a little help from Mae, they explored many topics—from dinosaurs to rocks, from insects to the Civil War.

Skip always walked Jimmy to the bus, opening the heavy school door and watching from the doorway until Jimmy was safely on. No one ever asked Skip to help Jimmy; he just assumed the responsibility.

Skip Letcher is now a successful businessman in the area. Recently, he told me that he still remembers sitting in the front of the room with Jimmy. They usually sat away from the other children so they could plan their many projects. He said Jimmy was a good student and he loved being his friend.

Minoa, like most schools, had those who felt that children like Jimmy didn't belong in a regular class. One teacher asked me why the little boy who coughs all the time is still in school. She felt it unfair for a teacher to have such a child in class.

Few knew that Jimmy got up at five o'clock every morning to prepare for school. Mae Ryan, his first teacher, knew it.

With tears in her eyes, she told me how he spent painful hours every morning getting ready for school. His most important preparation was using a machine that sprayed a powerful decongestant mist into his lungs. This mist loosened the thick mucus that had settled in his lungs, forcing him to cough up mucus so that he could breathe.

Even putting his clothes on was a tedious, excruciating process, but Jimmy was too independent to allow his parents to help him. His mother listened to Jimmy coughing painfully, and she knew how hard it was for him to even move in the morning, much less dress himself. She tried to help him on his first day of school.

Jimmy, with a flicker of anger in his eyes, said, "Mom! I'm not a baby."

"Jimmy, your dad and I only want to help."

"I know, but you have to remember I'm six years old. If I go to regular school, I must be like other kids and get ready by myself. If it is real bad, I'll call you."

The call meant that Jimmy was unable to rid his lungs of this thick, odious mucus by the inhalation of the fine mist. This meant his parents had to hit their child's back for sometimes up to a half hour to get him ready for school.

She pleaded with her doctor to find some other method to help Jimmy rid his body of the thick mucus.

She loved her doctor for he was a kind, sensitive man, but she felt that there had to be another way to help her son breathe. This sadistic procedure still angers her. She often asked Dr. Roberts for another method. He would shake his head, take a deep breath and tell her to pray for a cure as he does.

Jimmy would lie very still, never complaining as his mother pounded him. She always feared that Jimmy felt she was punishing him for having the disease. This insidious disease not only shortens the life of the child, but controls the life of all members of his family.

After that first morning, Jimmy's parents left him alone, but they could never sleep. They would lie awake in the adjoining room and listen to the choking, coughing sounds that were part of Jimmy's preparation. Only on his worst days did Jimmy miss school.

Every day was special to him. Jimmy's parents gave him an electric alarm clock for his birthday. Jimmy had been using an old wind-up alarm clock that ticked so loudly that they were afraid it might keep him awake.

Jimmy seemed delighted with the new clock, but when his mother noticed he was using both clocks, she asked, "Don't you like the new clock?"

"Yes, it is very nice."

"Why are you still using the old clock?"

Jimmy gave her a puzzled look. "But, Mom, what if the electricity went out at night? I'd miss a day of school."

Thirty years have passed since I last saw Jimmy, but our last day together is a memory that not only brings tears to my eyes, but also the memory of a child I will always cherish.

I was just finishing some paperwork when I saw Jimmy standing in the doorway of my office. I could see his chest heave as he struggled to breathe. He looked into my eyes and said, "Mr. Kinsella, thank you very much for letting me come to your big school."

He hesitated for a moment and added, "This will be my last day." He looked at me steadily, his blue eyes shining. My own eyes were misting over with tears as he turned to leave.

"Good-bye, Jimmy," I choked through the thickness in my throat. "I'll never forget you."

Breathing heavily, Jimmy looked up at my face. He turned to leave and then slowly turned around, flashed a weak smile, winked and left my office. He was dying and we both knew it. The mucus in his lungs had thickened to the point that it was actually suffocating him. A few days later, this courageous boy died.

Years have passed but memories and stories about Jimmy remain. I talked to Mrs. D. and her daughter, Elizabeth, a few years ago. We shared memories of Jimmy and discussed the great strides made in treating the disease today, including a test that determines if an unborn child will be born with cystic fibrosis. Her daughter, who was obviously pregnant, had declined to take the test. She had beautiful, healthy children.

But at the time, not knowing what would happen, she said, "I pray for a healthy child, but if my child is born with cystic fibrosis, I will love and cherish him every moment of his life."

She hesitated for a moment and then added, "Like my mom did with Jimmy."

CHAPTER 10

✍

Carly

Carly was a colicky baby. At least that was the designation every aunt in Donna's family made and it was reinforced emphatically by both grandmothers. These women were all immigrants and had nursed their children until they cut their molars. Donna, however, was a twenty-year-old first generation American. She married Anthony and had Joey before their first wedding anniversary. He was an easy boy to raise and Donna found plenty of willing hands in their extended family who'd care for him during the day.

She found a secretarial job at a large insurance company and was able to supplement Tony's salary. With luck, she thought, they'd be able to put aside enough money for a home of their own. They'd be able to leave the colony of caring, generous relatives and live their own lives.

It was an unwritten rule in their culture for the married children to settle in a flat in an area of the city devoted to their ethnic background. The elders of the family usually occupied the lower floor and the younger members had the walk-up apartments on the second or third floor.

Cozy, yes, but stifling. English was seldom spoken and customs from the old world molded the behavior of the children and grand-children before they reached school age. Then the first signs of questioning appeared and increased in succeeding years until full-scale rebellion began.

None of Donna's friends at school had ever heard of the evil eye and laughed at its power. She was told that she lived in an age of nuclear force and the superstitions of the past, like the evil eye, were for the gullible. Even the hold of the church was diminished and she listened more to secular voices, as did her husband, Tony.

Donna enjoyed her job. It was exciting to get up early, have her coffee and sweet roll, then turn Joey over to his grandmother and head to work. She was a pretty, slim, young, working mother who dressed in the fashion of the day. Her hair styles reflected the imagination of the finest salons. Her shoes were either high-heeled (three inches or more) making walking a precarious exercise, or so flat that at the end of the day her leg muscles were knotted and painful.

She did her own nails as an economy measure but otherwise she was officially an all-American girl, emancipated from tribal rites.

It was an inconvenience when she became pregnant again. She worked until her eighth month and sighed wistfully when her figure became rounder and nothing fit. Maternity clothes did nothing for her. She was bigger this time than with Joey and she retreated to her second-floor flat and counted the days until delivery.

Tony defied the elders this time and went to the Lamaze classes with Donna. He watched the delivery with wide-open eyes and when Carly was born, he knew that the warnings of the older folks were mumbo-jumbo. They said that men were not supposed to be witness to the event of birth. He knew it was a miracle—even though it happened millions of times each year. He felt that he was part of his daughter's life now. The hell with all those old wives' tales.

They found out that Carly was not a serene baby. Joey had spoiled them—he slept through the night after three weeks and even took two naps a day. Some of the forebodings of the women must have come true. The beautiful little girl would not quiet down, even if rocked or fed or burped. The nights were hopeless. They slept in shifts and wondered how long they could go on with two to three hours of sleep.

Joey had changed too. He had missed his mother during her lying-in period and wanted his share of attention. The baby was his rival and his father was not a substitute for Donna's tenderness and affection. The bewildered child would run through the flat, crying and added to the bedlam.

The young couple swallowed their pride and asked for a conference with the family experts. There was no doubt, they were told, that Carly had spasms or colic. They looked at Tony as if his attendance at the delivery was an affront to the gods of child rearing and the baby's behavior was a penalty for the transgression.

Remedies were recommended one after another; camomile tea, paregoric, honey and so forth. Nothing worked and at the one-month well-baby visit, Donna wailed out her story.

It is not uncommon for infants to have trouble adjusting to formulas. There is an immaturity of the digestive system in many infants that takes time to resolve. It does, in fact, last about three months and is a torment for families until the condition resolves spontaneously.

At Donna's request, a formula change was tried. Carly was switched to a soy preparation. She kept her despotic hold on her parents for another two days and then there was peace. Life was good again.

There was a blessed period of tranquility and Donna felt it was safe to return to work. Her family was willing to watch Carly while Tony and Donna continued their jobs.

Donna's mother loved holding her granddaughter. She would put her in her swing and sing to her during feeding. All the while Joey was playing with his trucks or nibbling on a cookie or two. Donna was called to an early-morning meeting at the insurance company and left without preparing the soy formula. At feeding time, her mother decided to improvise and reached for a can of ready-to-use Similac. Carly took the milk-based formula readily but within a few minutes after downing several ounces began to scream. She was picked up and patted and soothed without effect.

The baby's color became ashen. She was sweaty and was as floppy as a toy doll.

In a panic, her grandmother called Donna and met a busy line. Then she called my office and was told to bring the baby right over. They lived a short distance away and, although Carly was behaving strangely, her breathing was regular and she responded to her grandmother's reluctant pinch.

Fortunately, Carly had improved by the time she arrived at my office. Grandma's story of substituting the cow's milk for soy was the culprit. I advised Donna and Tony to see an allergist the same day. He verified the diagnosis and Carly was to be fed the milk substitute exclusively.

Just after Carly's first birthday an attempt was made to try a cow's milk challenge. The allergist added several drops of milk to her bottle of soy formula. He was prepared to manage any adverse reactions during the feeding experiment.

Gradually, additional amounts of whole milk were offered without ill effect. When the equivalent of six ounces had been ingested, Carly was considered to be tolerant of cow's milk once more and was sent home.

Donna was jubilant. When Tony called from work, the baby was sitting in her highchair nibbling on some dry cereal bits.

"Oh, Tony," Donna remembers saying. "Come on home as soon as you can and bring a quart of ice cream. Carly did great and can have an ice-cream cone at last."

She recalls that she stopped and looked at her daughter who had slumped forward in her highchair and was barely breathing.

Donna yelled into the phone, "Gotta go. Something's wrong with Carly!" In a panic she grabbed her and called 911. Her allergist met them in the emergency department as soon as they arrived. Carly was shock-like again. She was responsive but had a large bloody stool and was clammy, cold and pale again.

An IV was started and she gradually brightened up. No more cool milk on a summer's day . . . no chocolate candy bars . . . no yogurt or ice cream or cheese. The allergist determined that Carly had a delayed reaction to cow-milk protein. It affected her intestines primarily and any amount of a dairy product could reproduce the near-catastrophic results again.

On a scale of heroism, denial of the now-prohibited foods might appear a mild sacrifice. To Carly and her parents, the prospect of standing in the comer at birthday parties or other festive occasions and saying no to all the wonderful treats deserved the equivalent of a purple heart.

CHAPTER 11

❧

A Most Beautiful Bar Mitzvah

There was so much to learn. There were conditions that affected the children which had not been identified. It's not that there were new maladies, but my profession was so preoccupied with the major threats to life and normalcy—the outbreaks of polio and typhoid fever or tuberculosis, that our courses did not prepare us for the unusual.

One of the families in my practice was expecting again. They wanted this baby very much and hoped that it would be a boy this time. After three daughters they said that a son would put a finishing touch to their family. Of course, another girl would be loved but it would be nice to have a sloppy, tough little brother for the women to spoil.

Everyone got his wish. A nice broad-shouldered boy arrived and there was noisy celebration. He was destined to be given royal treatment from his many admirers. He certainly seemed to be without blemish and when I announced his weight and length and commented on his sturdy build there was glad acceptance of my report.

They named him Julius after one of his grandparents and hoped that he would be as fine a man as his forebear. The nursery was all decked out in blue and there were teddy bears and a rocking horse as well as a large toy chest filled with stuff that a boy would enjoy, just waiting for him to reach the right age. His father was counting the months until Julius and he would be able to do the things that dads and sons enjoyed. He had never played catch with his girls and felt isolated when feminine frills took the place of shooting hoops with a son.

Julius grew rapidly. He had doubled his weight in three months and his appetite was enormous. But he was not a baby who liked to be held or cuddled. And he made little eye contact but seemed to prefer being in his crib watching the whirling bird that made swooping movements when it was wound up. He'd watch it for hours but wouldn't look at his sisters or his mother when they reset the mechanical toy. He was a remote little being. He was contented to lie in his bed with a pacifier in his mouth, occasionally looking at his hands or rocking back and forth in some kind of rhythm, stopping only to be fed and then the cycle would begin all over again.

It was a puzzle for everyone. This beautiful little boy was a stranger in his own family. He didn't seem to notice anyone. His sisters wondered if he could hear and they cried when he didn't smile when they sang to him or tickled him. Finally they abandoned all efforts to get his attention.

His physical exam gave no explanation for his different behavior. I sent him for a hearing test and learned that he had normal responses. No one ever heard Julius make the gurgling baby sounds that most babies make. We were puzzled. It was as if he were from another planet and we were not able to communicate with him.

I searched the medical literature and stumbled on a paper from a psychiatrist from Johns Hopkins. Dr. Leo Kanner had reported on several children who had a condition that he called infantile autism; it sounded like Julius. There was no explanation for its occurrence. Dr. Kanner advanced some theories but nothing concrete and, more importantly, offered no recommendations for treatment. It certainly was odd but the description fit Julius.

It was 1949 and we were in unfamiliar territory. There weren't dozens of cases that had been studied. I suggested the parents find someone with greater experience than mine. After all this was the first case of this nature that I had ever seen. Together we tried to figure out a way to reach this little boy. The going was tough. Nothing worked. Julius grew as well as any other patient physically but he remained in his own secluded world, happy to play with spinning tops and key chains and totally indifferent to the dozens of treasures that filled his toy chest.

His family never gave up hope. There must be some place in this country where children with his bizarre behavior could be treated, they reasoned. Nursery schools were not able to manage his outrageous actions—sometimes withdrawn and at other times beyond control— unable to fit in. None of the mental health professionals were able to offer suggestions.

He would have to be cared for by his family; it was a daunting task. Julius' grandfather, Samuel, was the only one who could calm him down when he was frustrated or hyperactive. The old man would wait until the tidal wave of emotion subsided and then he would embrace Julius and in a quiet, soothing tone would defuse the crisis. They would sit together for a matter of minutes and Julius would find one of his wind-up racing cars or his music box and would lose himself in silent play. He had learned to operate the music box when he was four years old and had listened to it over and over. He would rock back and forth throughout the entire cycle, rewind it and remain entranced for hours.

Anyone who has ever dealt with a patient who cannot or will not communicate, knows that success is elusive. Parents cling to the hope that their child will emerge from the darkness and be whole again. They listen to the siren songs of the charlatans and try unproven, even dangerous remedies, always looking for a cure. Who can blame them when traditional medicine has little to offer?

Julius couldn't read but he loved to hear the same stories time and again. There were few people he would allow to even shake his hand or give him a reassuring pat on the back. His grandfather, was an exception. The boy would find a favorite book in the bookcase and would walk over to his grandfather's chair and motion to be picked up. Samuel would put his newspaper down and lift Julius onto his lap. The oft-told story would be read and Julius would remain silent to the end.

The next step was important. He would take the book from his grandfather, close it gently, place his cheek near the old man's lips and return the volume to the bookcase. There was a special bond between the generations. Samuel found the tie with his autistic grandson to be a cherished treasure.

During one of their evening story readings, Julius jumped up on his grandfather's lap, favorite book outstretched. Julius' hand brushed against the old man's face sending his glasses tumbling to the floor.

"Read, read," Julius commanded, as he opened the book. Samuel rubbed his eyes, and squinted at the familiar pages. He tried to capture his bifocals, but they had fallen several feet away.

He began, "Once upon a time." Julius nodded with each sentence until his grandfather paused, unable to recall the exact words in the fairy tale. He stumbled along until the impatient child put his hand over his grandfather's mouth and shouted, "No-no" and rattled off the entire story without an error.

Tears rolled down Samuel's cheek. He lowered the boy to the floor, retrieved his glasses and the two of them marched into the kitchen for cookies and warm milk.

Samuel loved his granddaughters intensely. They were able to weave their magic with uncanny skill and they had made the years following his retirement delightful. But they didn't need him as they bounced through nursery school, kindergarten, ballet classes, volleyball and first loves.

The only male left to carry on the traditions of his faith was lost in the confusion of autism. A man with three daughters and three granddaughters was the only one who was able to communicate with Julius. There was a chemistry between the two that was hard to define. The boy who was so distant with others, shadowed him wherever he went. Samuel had begun attending morning and evening services at his synagogue and his companion, Julius, was at his side daily.

The morning and evening services were the same each day, as they had been throughout the centuries. The prayers in Judaism, as in all established religions, have deep meaning for their followers and can be recited by heart by the faithful in time.

In a strange way the ritual was comforting for Julius. Most days of his life were spent duplicating what had gone before. Lack of variety was one of the features that set the autistic person apart from his peers.

The need for repetition made Julius a helpless student in the academic world. Lessons taught one day were the building blocks in most schools and as such were the stepping stones to the next level. His inability to adapt to change made formal education impossible. His vocabulary was limited to the few phrases needed to carry him through daily living.

Samuel was not an overly religious man. He observed the major holidays and an occasional Sabbath service. He and his wife did not keep a kosher home nor were they bound by other customs of the more orthodox congregations.

He had started attending the morning and evening services at his temple when he retired. It was more for the companionship of other men who missed the activity of their earlier years. He had never been able to find the time for civic affairs. Most working days had been spent in his general store where the many tasks of ordering merchandise, controlling inventory, overlooking his small staff and trying to keep up with his competitors, made time fly by.

After his daughters finished college and found husbands, he put his store on the market and prepared to enter the golden years of retirement. His wife was willing to have him spend hours in front of the TV set or with his nose in the *New York Times*. She encouraged him to play golf or join a bridge club; anything so her life could resume its former routine. She knew that retirement was a curse for him, not a blessing.

Samuel had been very athletic in his younger days. He had played basketball in high school and college but there had been little physical activity during the years before retirement. He was a tall, handsome man with a full head of white hair. He experimented with a beard and mustache at times but finally settled on a clean-shaven look. Although he had not gained much weight, the sedentary years had left him with a layer of fat around his midriff. With his daughter's consent, he bought a bicycle for Julius and after weeks of practice, his grandson was able to take his place on the bicycle trail.

Samuel kept pace behind him and the two cyclists could be found each day, getting in shape. Julius seemed to be freer and happier as they peddled through the hilly terrain of the county park. He was heart-broken when the weather cancelled their excursion, as it did altogether too often in their region.

Julius was nearing his thirteenth birthday. It was the time when boys become bar mitzvah'd and joined the ranks of their faith as a member of the synagogue. He couldn't attend the religious school to prepare for the traditional passage into manhood. His speech was lim-ited and he couldn't absorb the didactic lessons needed for a solo per-formance of portions of the Scriptures.

Samuel and Julius' parents spoke to the rabbi and asked to have a date set for Julius' bar mitzvah. It seemed absurd but the time was set aside six months into his thirteenth year.

Every afternoon after the outdoor exercise, Samuel and his grand-son put their bicycles in the garage, dressed neatly and went to the af-ternoon services. They sat in the back row of the small sanctuary and watched the behavior of the worshippers. When services ended, Samuel escorted him to the altar and the boy stood on a stool and faced the empty room. He saw where the Torah scrolls were placed and allowed Samuel to place a prayer shawl over his shoulders and a yarmulke on his head.

One of the shorter passages was assigned to Julius. It was to be sung in Hebrew when the candidate conducted the service. Samuel took advantage of his grandson's fondness for repetition and recorded the assigned passages on tape.

Night after night, with Julius at his side, they heard Samuel's voice sing the ancient words. Julius' favorite books were forgotten temporarily and remained on the shelf. Everyone was prepared for failure, but the planning went ahead.

Julius was outfitted in a beautiful dark-blue suit. He permitted his grandfather to select a white shirt and striped dark tie as well as black Oxford shoes. The day before his appearance in temple, Samuel sat his grandson down long enough to cut his hair. Strangely enough there was no struggle and the curls fell to the floor in a splendid heap.

The family arrived en masse. Father, mother, grandmother, sisters, the other grandparents and cousins. They occupied the front rows and waited nervously for the services to begin. The chapel was filled to capacity. Samuel had been given permission to accompany Julius to the altar.

Would the weeks of rehearsal be wasted? Samuel had a strange pounding in his chest as he stood beside his grandson. His lips were dry and his hands were shaking.

The preliminary prayers were recited and the Torah was unrolled. The rabbi placed the pointer on the passage for the morning. Samuel began to sing. He felt lightheaded and clammy. His voice was almost inaudible and then he stopped.

Julius turned toward his grandfather and shouted, "Sing, sing." Samuel did not make a sound. The rabbi looked at Julius and stepped back as the young man began to chant. He finished the passages in a voice that crackled as he reached the higher notes.

When he was done, he turned towards Samuel and waited for his reward—a kiss on the forehead. He was now a man in the eyes of the congregation.

CHAPTER 12

❦

Theresa

Theresa was only twelve-and-a-half years old when she came to me for her annual checkup two months earlier. She had been in good health and the visit was for a sports physical. A form had to be filled out by the private doctor with the parent attending or by the school physician. Both Theresa and her mother, Mary, preferred my office instead of the impersonal, more abbreviated, school exam. Her entire health record from birth to the present was in my files.

It was interesting to note that she weighed the same as she did more than a year earlier and her height was only a bit more. This was surprising because there usually is a growth spurt at her age.

I asked her if she had been sick since her last visit. The answer was no. Perfect school attendance and no complaints at all. How about activities was my next question. She was able to list a full schedule of clubs, chorus and sports as well as top-notch academics in the upper percentiles of her class.

This was the time in the life of a soon-to-be adolescent when body image was important. Many teenagers were so obsessed with appearances that they slipped into anorexia and flirted with disaster.

After a few other standard questions were answered to my satisfaction, I ventured into the appetite and diet area. Mary was puzzled about the weight but was insistent that Theresa was not skipping meals; not purging or cutting down on portions. She did not have a preoccupation with food or her figure and was quite content with everything in her busy life.

I proceeded with her exam. Everything was fine other than a little abdominal distention that I could not explain. She was sent to the lab for a bunch of blood and urine samples and we did a tuberculin test and asked her to return in several weeks for a follow-up examination.

Her weight was unchanged and there were no new symptoms. But her abdominal distention had increased considerably. The diagnosis was not apparent as yet but when we focused on the fullness in her abdomen and found that there was a fluid wave, it was imperative that we determine the cause of this abnormal finding. With their consent 1 asked for a consultation with several of my colleagues.

The gastroenterologist was disturbed by the presence of abdominal fluid and aspirated a large amount of a gelatinous material. This was followed by an admission to the hospital and a laparoscopic examination with a biopsy of a suspicious area of her intestine.

It was necessary to review all of the findings and discuss their significance with Theresa's parents. We found a conference room and began to talk about the biopsy report. The impact of this test result hung ominously over Theresa's future. There was no way to soften the words, "atypical cells, etc., etc." (pathologist's language). Mary was a nurse and was aware that her daughter's symptoms were dangerous. But there was a spark of hope and I was about to remove it. I had the complete report in my hand and I had to let the family know what was in store for Theresa.

My practice, like that of most pediatricians, usually dealt in happy endings. Most of the time we just stood back and let the natural course of events proceed unbothered. Perhaps that was one of the attractions of my specialty.

When the outcome was doubtful and a cloud hung over an entire family, it was heartbreaking. To be the messenger of bad news was the part of my duties that tore me apart.

The whole family was sitting in the conference room pretending to watch a large-screen television set. Mary, Big Dan, young Danny and Theresa were sitting on a sofa facing the TV screen when I came in.

Mary greeted me with a smile. Dan cleared his throat and said quietly, "Do you have the lab report yet, Doctor?"

I nodded. They scanned my face and knew I hadn't come with the words they wanted to hear. Theresa looked at her parents and then hugged them. No tears, no retreat. She had known all along that the fatigue and swollen abdomen and awful nausea had to be more than her body could overcome. How and why this had happened to her was a mystery. She couldn't give up now and she was prepared to do whatever was needed to defeat this thing.

She got up and went over to her brother. "Danny, will you walk me back to my room? Mom and Dad want to talk to the doctor."

Our discussion was brief and solemn. Dan and Mary had hoped that the biopsy would surprise everyone and be benign or at least amenable to treatment. Even this possibility was unlikely. The words "these various sections demonstrate the presence of an inflammatory myofibroblastic tumor which has undergone malignant transformation. Unfortunately, the prognosis is very poor for those inflammatory fibroblastic tumors which have undergone malignant transformation."

Medical jargon. A string of technical phrases that meant Theresa's chance of survival were negligible. Chemotherapy, radiation, more surgery would be employed while a search at every cancer center would be initiated in the hope that she would survive.

It is not in an oncologist's lexicon to say that there is no hope. Nor do the families want them to give up even though the therapy is filled with miserable side effects. Just to keep life going until a breakthrough treatment emerges is what drives both patient and physician.

Theresa was started on the first of the multiple drug protocols the next day. Her care was now in the capable hands of the Hematology/Oncology specialists. They were determined to give Theresa every possible chance to halt the spread of the malignancy.

There were other children in the section of the tumor center. Some had leukemia or brain tumors and there was a remarkable feeling of family among all of the patients. The staff knew that they were the last hope for most of them but they had a sense of history and could point to cures for a large percentage of childhood cancer cases. Twenty years earlier none had survived.

Theresa endured all of the procedures without complaints. There was no way to destroy the invader without having "chemo sickness." Symptoms such as nausea, vomiting, weakness, hair loss, mouth ulcerations, fever and anemia were invariable side effects of all treatment regimens.

The protocols called for a series of medications, then a rest period followed by more chemotherapy or radiation. She was unable to hold down nourishment with some of the scheduled treatment and needed parenteral nutrition to sustain her strength.

Whenever I visited her, she was upbeat and smiling. In her mind she figured that the suffering was worthwhile as long as she had a chance to be among the cured. Her weight seemed to melt away during the intensive anticancer therapy but she was determined to continue attending school. She looked drawn and pallid but when the bell rang at her high school, Theresa was standing in line, ready to complete a day away from the hospital.

She tried to attend gym classes but did not argue when the instructor led her back to her homeroom class. There was no falling off in her classwork, however. All of her assignments reached the teacher's desk on time, neatly done and worthy of her usual A's. The only concession that was made by her teacher was that she was allowed to wear her baseball cap in class, a violation of school policy. It masked her hair loss and kept her spirits up during the ordeal of intravenous drug therapy.

As the scheduled treatment went on, Theresa was able to take a number of trips through the Make-A-Wish Program. The respite time when one course was concluded allowed Theresa and her family to leave the horrors of treatment behind and lose the spectre of death. She was a wide-eyed spectator at Disney World, at Broadway plays, and enjoyed a cruise through the Hawaiian Islands.

The race to cram as many experiences as possible into one short life came to an end three years after the malignancy was discovered. She died at home with her parents at her bedside.

Services were held at a chapel not far from her school. I stood in line with hundreds of other mourners waiting to pay our last respects to Theresa. There was no need to hear a eulogy. The eulogy was her life and the way she faced death.

CHAPTER 13

❧

Nina

The phone rang in the den. A patient was looking for my father. I told the caller that I would relay the message and that he would be back to the office at seven p.m. Evening office hours after a long day were necessary. His once-busy medical practice was slowing down and he was worried about meeting expenses. Every patient counted. The caller was one of the loyal contingent who felt that my father was just as astute as before, even though his hearing was impaired. He still could deliver babies, sew up lacerations, diagnose diseases, and provide counsel for his patients. The new patients went elsewhere when he had them repeat their complaints in louder decibels.

I hated the next duty. He had come home for dinner and then lay down on the sofa for a short nap. He looked so relaxed, with a hint of a smile on his lips as if he were dreaming of better times. I gave him a little nudge but he didn't stir. He'd have to be awakened if he were to be in the office on time. A harder pinch and a rhythmic shaking of his shoulders aroused him. He looked up and nodded.

"Dad," I said, "Mr. Ferris has to see you this evening. I told him you'd be there on time. Sorry I had to wake you up. You were sleeping so peacefully."

He sat up, straightened his tie and headed for the washroom. I could hear him slapping water on his cheeks; heard him hum one of his favorite tunes and he was ready for his evening hours. Instead of a packed waiting room, the way it was in the past, some nights just one or two patients came in for care.

Deafness ran in our family. His mother never listened to our songs at birthday parties. She was a remote woman who was a silent statue in our memory. My father noted his own hearing loss when he was in his early thirties and each year it worsened.

Hearing aids didn't help him. The early models were conspicuous and he felt that they advertised that he was having trouble hearing what his patients were saying and so he abandoned them. He heard about a new procedure called a fenestration operation. He traveled to a specialist's office in New York City and returned defeated. He was not a candidate for the operation and would have to accept his handicap and watch his practice crumble. It broke our hearts to see him so despondent.

Years later when I was in a busy pediatric practice, I recalled some of the debates we had in medical school. A favorite discussion was centered around the senses of vision and hearing. Which presented the greater burden, loss of hearing or blindness? Usually far more young people felt that they could face the future better if they could see. They acknowledged the burdens of a world of silence but cherished the blessing of sight even more.

There was no way to appreciate the adjustments each of the sensory losses required. Children often pretended they were blind by covering their eyes with a handkerchief. They would bark their shins against the furniture or trip over a bunched-up carpet. That was the extent of their scientific experiment. Off would come the eye cover and the world would burst into view.

Over time, I encountered a number of children with the handicap of deafness or blindness. I had observed the impact on the life of an adult with hearing loss at close range and wanted, of course, to help someone born with this sensory deficit achieve communication skills.

There are many babies who are born prematurely in our country. The remarkable advances in newborn medicine, a field known as neonatology, allowed many tiny infants to survive. Some of them weighed barely more than a pound and after months of special care were struggling to overcome major defects.

Retinopathy of prematurity is associated with visual defects, occasionally total blindness. Small areas of bleeding in the brain of these tiny babies may end up with hearing loss as well as cerebral palsy. These children need all of the aid that medicine can offer. It is a triumph when the combined efforts of many professionals allow those with such handicaps to take their place in the classroom.

A good many of the deaf children have an entirely different problem. They are among those detected by the new screening tests that are performed in most nurseries in the country. These tests are able to find hearing loss or absence in the first days of life.

It is felt that the early discovery of congenital hearing loss will permit intervention and allow language acquisition and better educational opportunity for these babies.

I was not prepared for the refusal of one family to have their newborn tested. It was a full-term baby and they wanted to discover in their own way and at a later time whether their child was hearing impaired. The parents had become deaf early in life and felt that deafness was not a disability. They had learned to be part of a colony of others with similar deficiencies. They had their own language, their own sense of community and wanted their children, if deaf, to be part of their world.

There was no way that they would retreat from their position. Despite my experience with the hardship that deafness causes, I had to accept their wishes and not try to influence their thinking.

One child, a girl named Nina, was a beautiful little person. Her deafness was discovered when she was nearly two years old. There was no family history of an inheritable type of deafness and there was no explanation for her lack of hearing acuity. Her parents were extremely well educated with advanced degrees from college and she had an older sister who was a talented musician and an exceptional student.

For the first six months of Nina's life, her parents had no concerns. She loved the company of her family. She was an alert little infant with searching eyes and a constant smile on her face. She was seldom fussy even when wet or hungry. She was able to crawl by the time she was six months old and mastered standing and walking earlier than most. Her curiosity was a source of worry for everyone. Anything within reach would be found in her mouth unless strict precautions were taken and her mother had the poison center's number right next to the telephone.

Her sister, Fran, was four years older than Nina. She loved her baby sister and the minute she came home from nursery school would run in to play with her. She was the first to notice that Nina never babbled or made baby noises. Nina would just stare at Fran while she was playing peek-a-boo or making silly faces. She'd smile and kick her legs excitedly but never make a sound.

At first her parents thought it was merely a quirk of development. Surely a baby who seemed so perfect in every way would catch up. They could not continue their state of denial indefinitely. Fran had had an amazing vocabulary before she started nursery school and when Nina hadn't responded to the nursery rhymes or noticed the music box's melodies, their worries crystallized. They looked for help.

Nina was evaluated at the Speech and Hearing Center and her sister's observations were confirmed. The cute little child had sensorineural hearing loss and would need a special school for the deaf or she would be left behind despite her levels of attainment in all other areas of development.

She learned to sign easily and made lightning-like progress in the basics of communication. Her family hesitated to enroll her in the school for the hearing impaired in their area. They knew of the many advantages that it could offer but they preferred to have her stay at home with them rather than asking others to aid her in her communication skills. Even though she was isolated from other children of her own age, Nina was a normal little girl in most ways. She was a daredevil with her skates and her bicycle and suffered her share of bruises and cuts. She learned to use the computer and amused herself by the hour with video games and puzzles. Her life was busy and fast paced.

Her parents learned of a new procedure while searching the Internet. Cochlear implants had been introduced to the medical world in some research centers. Clinical trials had proven to be of great promise but had not been part of the practice of the specialists in their area.

Even though Nina had made such remarkable strides in the minds of her family, it was not enough. It would be worth whatever risk there might be and whatever cost they would incur.

Nina was the ideal candidate for the cochlear implant. She was young enough so that speech patterns could be achieved and that her world could be reinvented. It must be an experience beyond description to be able to hear music, wind, fire engines, and the tender sound from the once-silent lips of one's parents.

Fortunately, this new operation was successful. Nina and her family were able to communicate easily and she was able to have a life enriched with the wonders of symphonies and campfire songs and cheer with her friends at football games.

I never could resolve the debate of sight versus sound. There were many children in my practice who emerged from illness of prematurity or a genetic flaw who were "legally blind." They could be benefitted by some technological advances but nothing was comparable to the success of the cochlear implants for the deaf.

Nina was going to be able to reach any level her intellect would permit. No doors would be closed to her the way my father's handicap had changed his medical career.

CHAPTER 14

⟡

Megan

There are hundreds of children who crowd the pediatricians' offices every week. It is happy time for most parents. Their babies usually thrive and most of the time we just have to get out of their way and not interfere with Nature's plan. But a small number of the babies have problems of colossal proportions. That's the way it was with Megan.

The first time I saw her was in the newborn nursery. She was in a heated incubator because her temperature would not reach normal levels; her skin was blotchy and she was not very active. She was puny and her cry was a feeble whimper. She hardly moved when the nurse pricked her heel for a blood sample.

There wasn't much that I could add to that description. It wasn't unusual in the first hours of life for babies to be so lifeless. They are subjected to a traumatic voyage on their way into the world and the big surprise is that they rally so quickly most often.

Megan took her time. Her temperature finally stabilized and she was able to be taken to her mother for her first feeding. The baby showed little interest in nursing and her mother had to be contented to get acquainted with her daughter by degrees. Lisa skipped the feeding efforts and inspected her baby from top to bottom. Everything seemed to be in order. Ten fingers, ten toes, no birthmarks or unusual features.

She pressed the call button and was ready to have Megan returned to the nursery when the baby stopped breathing. In a panic, she screamed for help. A swarm of nurses and doctors raced to her room. The scene was tense until the medical team restored Megan's vital functions. Lisa hovered over the crib, finally reassured that Megan was all right. She was told that the baby would have to be observed in the special care unit for the next twenty-four hours but that she could visit as often as she wished.

The days stretched into three weeks before Lisa could take Megan home. She was a fussy infant and Lisa's days and most nights were spent holding her daughter and trying to fatten her up. Lisa cried when she bathed the baby and noticed her spindly legs and sallow color. She hoped that I would be able to give her some special formula or extra vitamins to spur her growth. In a way she was glad that it was winter and she wouldn't have to take the baby out for a ride in her carriage to endure the sympathetic remarks from the other mothers, the women whose babies were rosy-cheeked and plump. Maybe in a few months Megan would resemble the cute little daughter she'd always dreamed she'd have.

Megan's troubles were just beginning. Not only did she fail to thrive but she had episodes of vomiting and choking with her feedings. It was necessary to hospitalize her again when she had a series of seizures so severe that she needed intravenous anticonvulsants before they were under control.

Lisa stayed at the baby's side constantly; going home for a shower and a change of clothes and a cup of strong coffee. An electroencephalogram showed abnormalities often found in patients with epilepsy and the need to be on long-term medication was apparent. The therapy was effective in controlling her convulsions and Lisa was able to take her home once more to await the next blow.

There was a period of calm. Megan's growth began to accelerate and it was amazing to note the difference from one office visit to the next. Her hands and feet seemed to enlarge day by day and her head circumference increased so much that none of the baby bonnets fit her. Was it a result of her medication? Was it a hormonal abnormality? A disorder of the pituitary gland? It certainly was a mystery.

One of my pediatric textbooks is an encyclopedia of the unusual. The conditions in it are described in detail and there are photographs that reveal the appearance of each syndrome. It is a virtual gallery of the saddest of our population.

Megan, or a child who resembled Megan, graced one of the pages. She matched the words of the textbook closely. All of the features were there under the heading of cerebral gigantism or Soto's syndrome. No doubt about it. It was a fit. A forensic scientist would accept the data as incontrovertible proof.

Once the diagnosis of this rare condition was considered, it was necessary for Lisa to be told about the outlook for her daughter. I had never seen a child with Soto's syndrome and we had to review the literature together. The words, one by one, drove despair into Lisa. Megan's future seemed to be forecast in the paragraphs that stated there could be variable mental deficiency. With I.Q.'s of 18-119, with a mean of 72. Poor coordination. Hypotonia. Hyperreflexia. Delayed gross motor function. Significant behavioral abnormalities.

"Why bother to try to educate Megan?" the scholarly treatise seem to infer. There would be nothing but frustration and heartbreak in the years ahead if the gloom in the articles about the syndrome were correct.

Lisa hadn't spent years in specialty clinics compiling data and reporting all the negative features that might shape the life of someone with this handicap. She did know instinctively that Megan loved to be hugged and serenaded and made part of the family. She would know soon enough that she was different from other children and would have to be given the strength to endure the isolation that often came when you were one of a kind.

Lisa fought for her daughter from the moment that there was a diagnosis. She was not about to give up. Somehow she was going to help her child have a life as part of the community and not as a permanent resident in a treatment center for the hopelessly handicapped.

Megan was a frequent visitor to my office during infancy and early childhood. No serious illnesses occurred, just had to have her medication adjusted. Fortunately after three years she was able to be taken off of the anticonvulsant drugs. There had been no seizures since infancy.

It was a constant struggle for Lisa and Megan. There were years of looking for ways to stimulate Megan's interest in things other than food. The child's appetite was enormous but she had to be denied the gorging that she would do if left alone.

Every morning Lisa joined her daughter in an exercise routine. They had a specific goal. There was a park one mile from their home and Lisa set her stop watch and timed the round trip. She kept a record of their accomplishments and when they surpassed their best personal best, rewarded Megan with a gold star and a bag of popcorn.

The same tactics were used for school. Megan's attention span was fleeting, but she was made to exercise her mind as diligently as her body. Lisa would have made a superb Marine drill sergeant. Tears and alibis were ineffective. It was a sight to behold. The tiny mother, scarcely five feet tall and lost in a size four dress, had a plan for her daughter and let nothing stand in her way. Lisa decided to teach Megan at home. Home schooling had been very popular for many reasons but mainly for families who were dismayed by the breakdown of discipline and safety considerations in the public schools.

The curriculum was difficult for Megan to master but Lisa was relentless. She drilled her daughter in the basics of reading and beginner's math but handwriting was beyond Megan's capabilities. Her scrawl was illegible and it became apparent that she would need a different way of communicating. And so hours were spent with the computer until Megan learned to use it with some competence.

The child's vision presented a problem. She had a movement disorder called nystagmus which made it hard for her to fixate on objects. Her eyes would jump from side to side in rapid fashion. Glasses helped somewhat but the lenses were thick and the large frames gave her an owl-like appearance.

The home school curriculum gradually gave Lisa sufficient confidence that her daughter had mastered most of the skills of the elementary grades. It was time for her to join her peers in school.

Megan was placed in a special education class; ungraded at first. The contact with others in her age group was surprisingly successful. She looked forward to each day with enthusiasm and managed to do passing work. There was a flowering of her personality. The gawky youth had not become a graceful ballerina but neither was she an outcast.

There was a scheduled visit to my office several years after Megan had enrolled in the regular school system. Lisa accompanied her daughter and they waited patiently while the nurse helped Megan fit into one of our foolish paper gowns. When I walked in, I noticed there was an air of excitement and they had wide smiles on their faces.

Lisa handed me examination forms for working papers and for the Special Olympics. They had great news to share with me. Megan was in the tenth grade, as I knew already. She had been active on the swimming, skiing, and bowling teams and had won prizes in all of them.

"Doctor," Lisa said, "Megan wants to tell you something . . . wait until you hear it." She walked over to her daughter, raised Megan's arm as in victory. "Go ahead. He'll be so proud of you."

Megan's face flushed. "She was going to tell you. Well, here goes. I'm going to be one of the torch carriers for the regular Olympics."

Lisa interrupted. "There are only twenty-eight in the Torch Relay. My Megan is one of them. Each torch carrier has to cover two miles and pass it on to the next person. She'll be ready and I'll be running alongside her with my camcorder."

CHAPTER 15

᠕

What Developmental Delay?

Technology has changed our lives. Nowhere is that more obvious than in the practice of medicine. The use of the sonogram for the obstetrician is akin to the marvel of radar for the military. We are able to have a look at things that once were hidden. I remember the way we knew that there was an enemy plane or ship near at hand during World War II. It seemed like black magic at the time but the information we obtained allowed us to prepare a defense.

Nowadays, a couple no longer has to wait until the doctor eases the newborn into the world and have him announce, "It's a boy!" They can learn the sex and normalcy of the fetus in the first part of pregnancy and can prepare the nursery with the proper color and decor.

Unfortunately the glimpse into the future has its downside as well. If the shadows forecast trouble, the long months until delivery move very slowly.

Michael's mother learned that she would have another boy when her sonogram was done at four months. A second son, that was all right but the image on the screen also noted that his kidneys were enlarged.

Ellie had been one of my patients during the early years of my practice and had honored me by asking me to care for her firstborn, Tommy. He had been an easy child to rear despite a cluster of ear infections and the usual minor accidents. I would have to admit that she was an anxious parent with a focus on minutia. Many office visits were needed to reassure her that his migraine was not a brain tumor and that the green-apple colic was not appendicitis.

When she received the sonogram information, it was natural that she would look for reassurance from me as well as from her obstetrician. There was little that either of us could say to remove the cloud over her pregnancy. I promised that I would have a nephrologist available when the baby was born but told her that many times the sonogram is suggestive, not diagnostic of an abnormality.

Michael arrived on time. He had no evidence of kidney pathology after birth. There was a recommendation that a follow-up study be done at three months of age and that he should be treated as a normal infant.

He did very well at first. There was nothing to cause alarm but Ellie was not able to shake the feeling that Michael was not all right. His formula had to be changed several times because of spitting up and he had a fever with his first ear infection at five months of age. These common annoyances responded to treatment readily. There was one concern, however, that did need attention. Michael was not rolling over spontaneously and he was lagging behind in response to verbal stimuli and his head measurements were far larger than normal.

The combination of sluggish development and an enlarged head could not be ignored. Ellie and her husband had to wait and watch while Michael went through a neurologist's examination and a myriad of tests were run over and over again.

The consultant was as gentle as he could be but told the worried parents that their son was several months behind his peers in both motor and sensory development. He cautioned them that he might not reach the skill levels of his older brother. The good news was the although his head size was above the normal range, the MRI showed no structural abnormalities of the brain.

Ellie sheltered Michael with a protective shield. She deflected any suggestions that her son was slow. Her favorite phrase was, "We're not all alike, you know." She shared her pain with me, however. It was not in her makeup to accept the diagnosis of "developmental delay, etiology unknown."

She looked to me during his regular office visits to disagree with the other specialists and teachers. Michael certainly was different but there was a hint that he was catching up with his peers and I encouraged Ellie to continue working with him in the areas that showed promise. He had developed a vocabulary that belied his years. He was able to carry on a conversation with me that showed he was capable of reasoning, not just rote memory of silly TV commercials or nursery stories. There was logic in what he said and it gave us a glimmer of hope.

Preschool was a disaster. He was clumsy and poorly coordinated. His attention span was fleeting and he showed little interest in participating in the class activities but stayed by himself, contented to listen to the recording over and over and watch the hamsters run their endless marathon on their wheel . . . just like Michael . . . going nowhere.

I could not explain why Michael did not qualify for the label of developmental delay. His motor skills were of concern as he was quite klutzy; not a very scientific term but applicable in his case. He fumbled when he was asked to do a puzzle and wasn't able to hop on one foot nor could he catch or throw a ball with any skill. He was slow as well in learning to ride a two-wheel bike and couldn't climb a ladder. There were enough of what we call "soft" signs to place him in a handicapped category.

The look in his eyes refuted all of the negative test evidence. Somehow we were not reaching this boy and in my mind a different approach was needed. More time was needed before a verdict could be rendered about the best kind of school placement.

His parents heard all the gloomy forecasts and enrolled Michael in every one of the recommended courses. He didn't seem to fit any of the special training programs, but there was nothing else to offer.

It's hard to pinpoint exactly when the light turned on inside of Michael. He was still the slowest runner in his gym class and struck out nearly every time he was at bat. Maybe the karate lessons helped. It might have given him a feeling of self-confidence or it could have been that when he scored surprisingly well on the Iowa tests, that his teachers looked at him in a different light.

We discovered that Michael's interests were varied. He had a brief flirtation with dinosaurs and comic book heroes but abandoned these popular choices for an interest in bugs and rocks. He spent hours peering through his microscope or organizing his collection of fossils. His bedroom became a kind of Smithsonian Museum. He added new categories as his curiosity carried him down other pathways. Nobody dared to straighten up his room for fear of upsetting a special display.

Of course, the family was jubilant that Michael had awakened from his intellectual slumber. He still kept everyone other than his parents and his brother at a distance. I was confident that in time he would reach out and share his interests with those of his own age.

My hopes were realized when Michael came to my office for his annual physical examination. He was carrying some papers that needed my attention. There was the usual physical examination form as well as a magazine. After I completed my exam and signed in the proper places, he handed me the magazine. It had a paper clip attached to one page of his school's publication.

Michael had been elected to the Honor Society for academic

achievement. He had written a poem that had won a place in the annual selection of outstanding work by seventh grade students.

He smiled as I read the following lines and then joined his parents in the waiting room. His poem does not suggest that he is another Keats or Shelley but it won a round of applause from me.

I WILL LOVE YOU FOREVER

I love my mom with all my heart,
When it comes to homework she is very smart.
She cooks my food and irons my clothes,
And even takes care of my bloody nose.
Some people think she's as old as a willow,
But me, I think she's as cool as the other-side-of-the-pillow.
She really is a bright shooting star,
I know she is the best by far.

My forecast for the future was far rosier than the prenatal sonogram and MRI. Maybe Ellie could stop worrying at last.

REPORT CARD
Seventh Grade

Class	Teacher	1st Marking Period
BAND	DeGroff	94

Michael is a pleasure to have in class.

Class	Teacher	1st Marking Period
ENGLISH 7L	Baldwin	98

Michael's attitude in class generally excellent, shows outstanding interest.
Michael's homework assignments regularly in on time.

Class	Teacher	1st Marking Period
H&C 7FL	Dombrosky	97

Michael accepts responsibility and completes work promptly.
Michael's attitude in class generally excellent, shows outstanding interest.

Class	Teacher	1st Marking Period
MATH 7AL	Petrie	100

Michael's attitude in class generally excellent, shows outstanding interest.
Michael accepts responsibility and completes work promptly.
Michael is a pleasure to have in class.

Class	Teacher	1st Marking Period
PHYS ED 7	Jones	100

Class	Teacher	1st Marking Period
SCIENCE 7L	Fusco	95

Michael is able to work independently.
Michael's homework assignments regularly in on time.
Michael's attitude in class generally excellent, shows outstanding interest.

Class	Teacher	1st Marking Period
SOC. ST. 7L	Painter	98

Michael's quality of work was excellent this marking period.
Michael's attitude in class cooperative and attentive.

Class	Teacher	1st Marking Period
SPANISH 1	Howell	100

Michael is a pleasure to have in class.
Michael's quality of work was excellent this marking period.
Michael's attitude in class generally excellent, shows outstanding interest.

Times Absent:	0
Times Tardy:	0
MP Average:	97.78

CHAPTER 16

❧

High Tide

The hurricane season was over. It had been more severe than usual and damage to waterfront property ran into the hundred of millions of dollars. The shoreline at their favorite beach was strewn with litter and activity was at a standstill. At this time of the year the population of their small coastal town was usually two or three times its usual size. The natives hated to part with their privacy but they depended on the tourist trade for much of their income.

The skies were still forbidding—dark promises of more rain and a cold wind that penetrated through down jackets and colored noses and ears with a scarlet tinge. Some of the usual guests had cancelled their reservations already and many of the bed and breakfasts were forced to furlough their staff.

The town hadn't changed much over the years. There wasn't a row of fast-food eateries or movie houses or taverns. Just two grocery stores, the town library, the high school and the companion elementary school down the block; the Methodist Church and the Catholic Church with its beautiful painted glass windows and tall spire. The doctor and the dentist shared a building on the main street. There was a gas station on one corner and a garage and Chevrolet showroom on the other. The fire barn and the town's ambulance were near the post office and the headquarters for the three-man police force made up the rest of the official civic buildings. There was a village square as well with monuments to fallen heroes of the wars of the past two centuries. There was a solitary building fifty yards away from the square where the meeting hall had been built near the turn of the century. It overlooked the other structures and housed the offices of the town clerk, the county judge and the district attorney for the region.

Marshall had searched for a town that time forgot for many years. This tiny seacoast village had the extra features that made it the ideal refuge for him, his daughter and grandson. It was a dot on the map with a permanent census of less than two thousand. Not a place for nomadic retirees looking for a warm paradise that replicated the busy life they had enjoyed in earlier years.

He had different needs. His island of tranquility had to be within driving distance of a medical center. His grandson, Eugene, had a progressive neuromuscular disorder called type II spinal muscular atrophy, also called Wohlfart-Kugelberg-Welander disease. It was not curable and it made its way relentlessly with slow bites on nerve endings and synapses. By degrees the victims were unable to do much more than merely survive.

The long wait for favorable weather was disturbing. The drizzle and unseasonable chill erased Marshall's chances for an outing with Eugene. Last year they had been at the beach nearly every day. There was a favorite spot, not far from the shore with a covered shelter, a fireplace, some picnic tables and a drinking fountain. The view of the ocean was magnificent and the two of them would sit for hours, watching the gulls swoop down on the fish or they'd just gaze at the waves as they crested and rolled onto the shore.

Often Marshall's daughter, Jeanne, joined them. That was before Eugene was confined to a wheelchair. There were at least twenty-five snapshots in their album, showing Eugene nibbling a hot dog or enjoying a toasted marshmallow.

But the weather was not their only enemy. The spinal muscular atrophy had forced Eugene into wheelchair dependency. His chest muscle weakness made breathing more difficult and even chewing and swallowing were trials.

Eugene had many interests. He loved to read and books about fishing, boating and mountain climbing were his favorites. Stories of adventure filled his bookshelves. Each one transported him from his imprisonment to lands he'd never see, rivers he'd never ford, thrills he'd never experience. But his eye would be riveted to the pages of journeys into space or to the center of the earth. Jules Verne, Robert Louis Stevenson and J. R. R. Tolkien fed his fantasies and helped overcome the monotony of the sickroom.

Jeanne entered his bedroom early one morning. "I just heard the weatherman say it would be clear and sunny for the next few days. At last, huh, Gene? Gotta get you and granddad ready for one of your trips." She looked at her son, such a little boy with an awful disease.

He and her father had come back from fishing last year with enough fish to fill her freezer. They were quite a team. Marshall would bait the hook and Eugene would drop the line into the water and wait expectantly for his catch. He'd feel the tug and yell to his grandfather for help. Both fisherman were jubilant with their success.

How would they fare this year, she wondered as she lifted her son out of bed and dressed him for his first outing of the season.

The doctor at the medical center had warned her that Eugene had regressed over the last few months. Not only did he need the wheelchair but he required help in breathing. His chest wall excursion was feeble and he needed oxygen more and more often.

His wheelchair was an astonishing piece of equipment. It was motorized and he had learned to operate it readily. There was a space for the oxygen cylinder and the lightweight face mask was within easy reach. He liked to pretend that he was driving an Indy 500 car while Marshall walked behind him on their way to the waterfront. Imagination translated the five-mile-per-hour pace of his motorized chariot into the final turn at the racetrack and a chance for the checkered flag.

They reached their destination and Marshall helped Eugene position the wheelchair near the water. The beach was deserted despite the break in the weather. Not even a solitary stroller or hopeful fisherman.

Marshall was an imposing figure. He had gained a few pounds since his years with the NYPD but he was still interested in regular workouts. Every morning, rain or shine, since his move south, he donned jogging clothes and ran at least four miles. His thick head of hair was a mixture of black and silver. He had a full mustache but no beard.

He loved to cook and he and Jeanne had a clear separation of responsibility in their bed-and-breakfast undertaking. He was in charge of the kitchen. He ordered the supplies, planned the breakfast menu, made the omelettes and sausages and waffles, brewed the coffee, served the guests and was responsible for the cleanup.

Jeanne's role was that of the manager of everything else. She took care of the patrons' sleeping comfort, the furnishing of the hundred-year-old house, the gardening and the hiring of the domestic help.

In-between times, each of them shared Eugene's care. There were exercises and massages and more recently breathing exercises. Eugene was the ideal patient with no complaints and filled with determination to improve, to achieve an immediate goal of independent walking again.

Marshall and Eugene passed the long hours of therapy with baseball trivia contests. Each of them was a dyed-in-the-wool sports fan. They knew everything about the Yankees and Eugene's room was filled with memorabilia and autographed pictures of his idols. But their knowledge was not Yankee-thin. They challenged each other with questions from the Ty Cobb era to that of Hank Aaron and Derek Jeter.

They enjoyed teasing Jeanne by exposing her ignorance. "Mom," Eugene asked her one day, "what team did Babe Ruth play on before he was traded to the Yankees?"

She never knew the right answer and Eugene's glee was abundant. He'd turn to his grandfather and gloat. "Girls don't know much about important things, do they, Grandpa?"

Eugene sat in his wheelchair while Marshall prepared the bait. They chose mullets for the morning's fishing. The fish would be eager for his attractive food, he was sure, just as they had been in the past.

He gave the lightweight rod to his grandson and helped him cast his line. Eugene found it hard to hold the rod and suddenly it slipped from his grip.

Marshall consoled the unhappy boy. He went to retrieve the rod but lost his footing and fell into the water. He tried to brace his fall but was thrown against a rock by a towering wave. He was unable to right himself. His trouser was ripped and his leg was badly damaged. Marshall tried to pull himself toward the shore but the undertow was too strong and he could not advance toward safety. The pain was intense and he hoped that he would not lapse into unconsciousness. He didn't know how he could be rescued.

Eugene didn't panic. He reached into the pocket of his wheelchair. He lifted the cell phone, making sure he had a secure hold and dialed his home number. He looked out to where his grandfather was lying helplessly in the water.

"Please, dear God, let her be there instead of out shopping," he thought to himself. After several rings, he heard his mother's hello.

"Mom, Grandpa's hurt and bleeding. It's real bad. He fell against a rock while we were fishing. Get the ambulance right away." He started to cry. "I'm of no use. I can't do anything to help him."

Jeanne came racing to their fishing spot in her recreational vehicle. The town ambulance followed close behind. Two of the ambulance crew hurried to where Marshall was lying; half-submerged in the water. He was still conscious but in obvious pain. They carried him gently to the shore and lifted him onto a stretcher.

Marshall looked over to his grandson and his daughter. He gave Eugene a thumbs-up sign and said, "Ask your mom who was the last big league ballplayer to bat .400."

Jeanne ran over to her father and kissed his forehead. She watched as they lifted the stretcher with Marshall into the ambulance and headed to the hospital. Then she shouted as he was leaving.

"I'll look it up on the Internet." She turned to Eugene. "Come on, my hero, let's go home."

CHAPTER 17

❧

A Gift of Life

Lacrosse was his passion. John grew up in a part of the country where teams began their rivalries in pee-wee leagues and continued to battle for recognition into their college years.

John was my patient from his first cry at delivery until the examination for college entrance. He was a good student, fortunately, because much of his attention was focused on lacrosse. Our region has pretty harsh winters and it was hard to practice outdoors from Thanksgiving to Easter. He and his equally dedicated friends braved the elements as they perfected their skills until their fingers were frozen and their cheeks were numb.

When they were forced indoors, the practices continued although some of the flavor was gone. It is an uncontested claim that this splendid game was originated among the Native Americans in our state. Whether or not it is factual, many of the high schools and colleges in this part of the country consider lacrosse to be their major sport.

At one of his sports physicals during his sophomore year in high school, I noted that his blood pressure was elevated. He had had no illnesses during the year and everything else was normal. He was advised to return every several months for further testing. No restrictions were placed on his activity.

His blood pressure remained higher than we liked and he began to show protein in his urine. There was no change in his energy though. He was referred to a kidney specialist and a battery of tests showed that he had a form of nephritis that required careful monitoring and medication to manage his blood pressure.

John was a diligent patient and followed the nephrologist's recommendations as best as he could. Lacrosse was not forgotten, though, and he enjoyed the success of his team in the regional tournaments.

The disease process in his kidneys appeared to be under control. His mind turned to other things and he applied to college. He managed to find a school where academics and lacrosse could co-exist. He packed his bags for the next adventure and left the area. His brothers kept me informed over the next few years whenever they came to my office for care. John stopped in to see me once during a school vacation. He had bulked out a bit but seemed fit and he told me that he felt great. He hadn't bothered to see a doctor, just had a visit to the team physician for a sports-related injury.

It was early in his senior year at college that his mother called me. John had failed his sports physical, she told me. His urine showed a greater amount of albumin; his blood pressure was elevated and his kidney function was twenty percent of normal. He had end-stage glomerulonephritis, a term indicative of an advanced degree of kidney damage.

The next months were harrowing for John. He dragged himself to class—just trying to finish his courses so he could graduate. The lacrosse stick was packed away and he joined the ranks of thousands of others waiting for an organ transplant, meanwhile undergoing dialysis.

The rest of this story is taken from the Syracuse newspapers. There was an article that appeared about this family.

"Son Thanks Mom for Gift of Life"

Hours after doctors transplanted a healthy kidney into his abdomen, John Prior fought the pains to step gingerly out of his hospital bed and, in the process, was reborn.

"If you feel like getting up over the next few days, you can," the nurses had said, but Prior shot back, "Let's do it now."

"After the transplant I felt mentally and physically well-oiled," Prior, 22, recalled. "It's really the weirdest feeling I ever had. . . . You feel incredible, getting this second chance."

Prior's mother, Rose, groggy from major surgery of her own, watched from the hospital bed as her firstborn son took tentative steps from his, and in the process was reborn, too.

Nearly eight months after Rose Prior donated a kidney to John, the pair celebrate Mother's Day today at their home in

Shotwell Park in Eastwood. John has a second chance at a healthy life, and Rose is convinced she's blessed with the best gift a mother could have.

"When I saw him walking that day after our surgery, I felt like I had truly given him life again," Rose said. "I said to him, 'John, now you have two birthdays.' I'd told the doctors, 'Take whatever you need.' I'd have given him my life."

Rose Prior of Syracuse is one of more than 2,000 Americans who donated a kidney to an ailing relative last year. She is part of a growing number of parents, children—even grandparents—who are the donors in what doctors call "living donor transplants."

In the United States, about one third of all transplanted kidneys are taken from living relatives of the patients, because a relative is more likely to have tissue compatible to the person who is sick.

Last week, John called the National Kidney Foundation of Central New York, looking for a Mother's Day gift suitable for a mother who donated a kidney.

The office is stocked with "I LOVE YOU WITH ALL MY KIDNEY" bears and mock kidneys made of soft plastic that you can squeeze when the stress kicks in, but none seemed worthy of this mother's sacrifice.

So John decided that he might begin to repay the debt by telling his story. "My mom's my hero, and to so many other recipients, their donors are heroes, too," John said. "Just by signing the donor card on your driver's license, you can be a hero"

If John hadn't been fortunate enough to have received his mother's kidney last September 20, he might be among the one hundred twenty Central New Yorkers currently waiting for a kidney transplant.

Each day in this country, thirteen people die awaiting an organ transplant, said Marion Makuli, executive director of the National Kidney Foundation of Central New York. Too few potential donors know how their organs can benefit other people after they die.

"The message we want to get out is that it's not enough to

merely sign a donor organ card," Makuli said. "You must tell your next of kin about your wishes. You could have ten cards lined up in your wallet, but unless you communicate your wishes, doctors can't take your organs."

Because almost everyone is born with two kidneys, a kidney is the only organ that living donors can give to an ailing relative. Live donor transplants have the added benefit of higher survival rates than transplants with kidneys donated from cadavers, according to the National Kidney Foundation headquarters in New York City.

John, an accomplished lacrosse player and regular runner, never thought he'd need a transplant, let alone a transplant at such a tender age. He felt immortal, completely unbeatable, "like nobody could take me."

But as a junior at Henninger High School, John was diagnosed with high blood pressure, and doctors looking for kidney disease could never uncover a cause.

John continued to play lacrosse in college. Then, as he was about to begin his final semester at State University College at Oswego, his world caved in. You're in kidney failure, the doctors told him.

"We felt powerless, devastated with the news," Rose recalls. "But John went right back to school like a trouper, and had his best semester ever. And he made me carry on."

From the beginning, John asked the doctors to sustain what little kidney function he had left with medications so he could graduate from college without kidney dialysis. The goal, he said, was to hold out for the transplant without being tethered to a machine.

He prevailed—at least until graduation, a victory he called "bittersweet." Yet John felt worse and worse last summer. He still hoped to avoid dialysis, and did not always level with the doctors with how much he vomited or how rotten he felt. Five weeks before his transplant, he couldn't put dialysis off any longer.

From early on, it looked like Rose was the best candidate to donate one of her kidneys. With every medical test she passed—doctors screened her for everything from lupus to infections—she felt more and more elated.

"You take care of your children from day one, and when something like this happens, you feel out of control because it's something you can't fix," she said, "I was never so thankful as the day I found out I could give him a kidney."

Still, John resisted. "I thought I'd rather wait on a list than take her kidney," he said. This time it was his mother's turn to prevail.

When the two headed into surgery at the Albany Medical Center last autumn, they benefited from a half-century of medical science. In the 1950's, doctors learned they could transplant kidneys, but such transplants invariably ended in failure because patients' bodies rejected new organs.

In the 1960's, doctors discovered that corticosteroid drugs and some anticancer agents suppressed the body's rejection response. In the 1980's, the introduction of an immunosuppressant drug called cyclosporine improved the success rates for transplant surgery even more.

Still, Rose, a devout Catholic, prayed every day.

She prayed on the car trip to Albany, and she prayed with John in the wee hours the morning of the surgery. In a small chapel near the hospital, they knelt and prayed again.

Before she was wheeled into the operating room, Rose gave her youngest son, Andy, thirteen, a cherished rosary ring for safe keeping. John, his eyes wet, hugged his seventeen-year-old brother, Mark, and pledged to whip him in a future game of golf.

For more than seven hours, Rose's husband, David, and their two younger sons passed the interminable wait in the halls of Albany Medical by pacing and praying and pacing some more. When Rose finally emerged from the recovery room, David whispered to his wife, "You did it. John's OK."

Even before the surgery, John adopted the attitude of a warrior, telling himself he was entering what he called "the fight of my life." His first gingerly steps in the hallway outside his mother's hospital room were a major victory.

But there were other battles ahead.

Two months after the surgery, a nagging little itch in John's chest turned into an excruciating pain. Doubled over, John went to the emergency room, where doctors diagnosed a virus that would have triggered a minor ailment in a person whose immune system wasn't suppressed.

As fall turned into winter, John spent eight weeks in the Albany Hospital, and he felt both his confidence and hope flagging.

This time it was David's turn to step up. While Rose stayed at home with their other sons, David stayed by John's bedside late into the night.

"You can do it if you keep on," he told his oldest son. "I know you can do it."

John's competitive edge kicked in, and he rallied.

"Everything I've succeeded in," John said, wiping his wet cheeks and nodding at his parents, "is because of them"

Most of this story is by permission of the Syracuse Newspapers. It is from a feature story on Mother's Day on May 14, 2000, from the Sunday *Herald American* by Melanie Gleaves-Hirsch.

CHAPTER 18

∽

Solly

His father pronounced him dead. There was no way he could be convinced that Solly was not a cruel joke of Nature. He refused to listen to his wife when she begged him to accept their son in spite of his life style. Alex was a powerful man with a thunderous voice that made Solly quake. The welts that covered his back faded within a week after his father punished him but the isolation never disappeared.

Alex and Sophie had left the Ukraine shortly after their wedding. They had found a small community of their countrymen in our city and blended quickly in their new home. There were numerous jobs in the factories that studded the area. Alex began work at one of the steel mills near the lakeshore and spent his hours feeding coal into the blast furnaces. It was a dirty, strenuous chore but Alex loved the physical labor, the good pay and the camaraderie of the other men.

He and Sophie bought their first home the year before Solly was born. It was a few miles from the factory in a little settlement of modest houses. They were all similar on 40'x100' lots; three bedroom cottages with room for a garden, a garage and a workshop.

Alex loved to tinker with anything mechanical, from refrigerators to the second-hand car he bought from a friend. He spent hours on the weekends rebuilding the engine, washing and polishing his old Chevy until it was in nearly showroom condition.

Once a week when it was his turn to carpool, he would pile his friends into his car, drop them off at work, and park as far away as possible from others in the lot. He wanted to avoid dents and scratches that might scar his prized possession. When the whistle ended their day, Alex would complete his once-weekly ritual. There was a stop at his favorite tavern and he would host his friends to a round of drinks while they played a few games of pool.

Life was good in this land of opportunity. Sophie missed her family, of course, but there was so much to do and learn, that she had no regrets about leaving her homeland. Maybe someday her parents and brother and sister would join them.

Sophie's garden kept her busy all spring and summer. The rows of vegetables ended up in their pantry at harvest time with jars of beets, carrots, zucchini and dill pickles—favorites of Alex's—ready to round out their winter menu.

She was excited when Alex found a Singer sewing machine at a garage sale shortly after she learned that she was pregnant. She turned her attention to making her maternity clothes and curtains and other accessories for the nursery.

Alex's first look at his son was typical of most fathers. He was awed and frightened. This seven-and-a-half-pound newborn would need his guidance and love. He could hardly wait to tell his friends about the baby and shove a box of cigars in their direction and receive good wishes. Then he sent telegrams to his relatives back in the Ukraine.

Solly was a placid baby, no problem at all for Sophie. She nursed him until he was two years old and his sister, Olga, arrived. He trudged after his father, mimicked Alex's mannerisms and enjoyed being a central part of his father's life.

Nothing changed when Olga was born. Sophie found time for both children while Alex found excuses to concentrate on Solly. He wondered if his son would follow in his footsteps and work with his hands or perhaps find a spot in industry at a level he could never reach himself. To have his son become the first one in the generations of his family to go to college was a dream he hoped would come true.

Alex loved to march around the neighborhood with Solly hoisted on his shoulders. His face would light up as he bragged to everyone about his son. He'd try to make the boy recite a poem in two languages and would bribe him with Hershey bars if he balked. "He is the future," he'd say. "He'll be somebody. Just listen to him. He's only three and a half. Do you know he can count up to forty already?"

It was harmless or so it seemed. How many parents have budding geniuses who delight them with their precocious skills only to learn that countless other children are just as gifted?

Alex and Sophie joined the Ukrainian Church when they settled in the U.S. Much of their social life centered around the church. When Solly reached school age, Alex insisted that he attend the parochial school even though it strained their budget. It was an all-boys school and was noted for its academic excellence. They decided that Olga would stay in public schools and transfer to the parochial school.

Solly was an apt student with grades among the highest in his class. His tastes were eclectic, ranging from language and math to arts and drama. He was a serious boy who spent most of his free time in the library or practicing his violin (which he played poorly). To his father's disappointment he did not try out for any of the high school teams; didn't even use his free athletic tickets for his school's championship run.

Solly was taller than most of the boys in his class. He had thick blond hair and handsome features. His smile came easily and although he had few close friends, there was a classmate who shared many interests with Solly. They liked to hike up to the hills overlooking the city and would sit on the grass near the water tower discussing the problems of the world. The main topic was the Vietnam War which had become a quagmire for young Americans.

Sophie and Solly were busy preparing for the school play. The ninth grade actors had been studying their parts for days and Sophie was putting the Singer sewing machine to good use. Solly's costume was ready a few days before the performance. He was anxious to see his image in the mirror and imagine how he'd feel when the curtain went up and he faced the audience. Would he forget his lines? Would he be able to stop his knees from shaking? Would he stumble over his flowing robes as he crossed the stage?

Sophie straightened out his costume and asked him to stand in the dining room near the large picture window. She ran for her camera and used most of the roll with Solly in various poses. Then she helped him remove his costume, folded it carefully and placed it in a large suitcase.

She looked at her tall, handsome son. "Your father and I will be sitting in the front row tomorrow night. We'll celebrate after the show. How about it? Just the four of us . . . unless of course the whole cast has something planned."

Solly smiled. "Sounds great to me. There's nothing scheduled as far as I know. Yeah, I'd like that a lot."

The annual play was a period piece set back several centuries ago. Solly was the queen who was beloved by her subjects but was the target of a plot against her life by a dissident faction.

Solly made his appearance, resplendent in his royal costume. He had long earrings, cheeks touched up with rouge, mascara'd eyes, jewelry befitting his station and a crown. He spoke in the falsetto he had practiced for days and held everyone's attention throughout the evening.

The applause when the curtain went down was long and gratifying. The actors were called back several times for more recognition.

Alex sat in the first row of seats. He saw his son appear in the leading role, portraying the queen of a fictitious kingdom. He turned to Sophie and hissed, "Why didn't you tell me what he was doing? How could he disgrace us like this?" He turned and ran out of the theater.

It was quiet when Solly, Sophie and Olga came home. There were no lights on in the parlor. Olga saw that Alex was sitting in his favorite easy chair. He had a heavy rope in his hand. He was twirling it back and forth.

"Daddy, you scared me," said Olga. "Sitting like that in the dark. We wondered why you left before the play was over. We were going to have a little party in Solly's honor."

He pushed her aside and grabbed Solly by the shoulder. Alex was breathing heavily and he began to rain blow upon blow on Solly's back and arms.

"Maybe this will teach you how to act like a man," he shouted. "When you feel some pain, you'll know what you've done to me. I've lost a son and got me I don't know what. A queer. Just like that damn kid you've been hanging around with."

Alex struck him again until Sophie came between them. He threw the rope to the ground and ran out into the night.

Sophie brought her son to my office the next day. The injuries were ugly but Alex's violent behavior was uglier.

I spoke to Solly alone and was surprised when he told me he was relieved in a way that his innocent portrayal had exposed his father's intolerance. He said that for years he had liked to dress in his mother's clothes and pretend that he was a woman. No one had caught him with his cross-dressing. It was a feeling he couldn't control, he said.

I told Solly that his father had deeply-held beliefs, and that his intolerance was wrong but was a product of his heritage. Alex enjoyed the tough talk, the hikes, the fun with the other men at the tavern. He watned Solly to be cast in his image.

Gender identification disorders are difficult to manage. Alex refused to discuss the issue with me and repeated that his son was lost to him. He would allow Solly to live with them but he would be a stranger from now on.

They seldom talked. Solly tried to explain his feelings to Alex but was met with stony silence. Solly finished high school as valedictorian of his class, but decided that he would defer plans for college.

The Vietnam War had escalated into a major conflict with no end in sight. Solly joined the Army right after his eighteenth birthday and was shipped overseas after a short training period.

His tour of duty exposed his unit to some of the worst fighting of the war. Casualties were high on both sides and after three months of combat, Solly was hit by shrapnel and was evacuated to the base hospital. His right leg was shattered and could not be salvaged.

When Alex and Sophie visited Solly in the hospital, they saw him in a wheelchair in the midst of other wounded soldiers.

Alex looked at his son, threw his arms around him and exclaimed, "Welcome home, Solly. You came back a man!"

CHAPTER 19

❧

Adele

There is so much happening in stem cell research and cloning experiments that it is interesting to turn back the clock and see where we were forty or fifty years ago.

In September 1938 my medical school accepted forty-eight students. We entered this new world with the hope that we would reach our goal and become doctors. The curriculum was loaded with difficult courses and demanded a type of dedication most of us had never faced before. Hours spent in the anatomy lab were followed by equal time every night with our noses buried in *Gray's Anatomy*. Or the world of histology with a different approach to the study of man as seen through the microscope.

Our anatomy professor was an impressive teacher. His lectures were awe-inspiring. He would stand with his back to the class and fill the blackboard with diagrams. He would hold a yellow-colored chalk in one hand; a plain white chalk in the other and sketch the liver with his left hand and the spleen with the right. All the while explaining the details of one structure or other. It was a performance no one ever forgot, even though the specifics of the exercise may not have remained in our minds.

This man was tall, lean and was in constant motion. His light blue eyes could burn a hole through a student during an unscheduled oral exam. His quarry would be selected at random; his finger would point at his target and his eyes would penetrate deep into his victim's knowledge base. It was analogous to a tiger cornering a gazelle. The rest of the class watched and prayed that they would not have their weaknesses exposed at a later date.

He was nicknamed "Pussyfoot"—a well-deserved sobriquet. He liked to walk through the anatomy lab in an aimless fashion and stop suddenly at a table, grasp a branch of a nerve and say, "What is the name of this nerve and what area does it supply, Doctor?" We were in his eyes pathetic pretenders and it was his duty to make us raw recruits into professionals.

There was a sharp contrast in the teaching style of the histology professor. There was no intimidation; just an earnest desire to have his students share some nuggets of wisdom with him. He was approaching retirement. For thirty years he had taught the same course. His lab coat was rumpled with note paper and pencils in each pocket. He no longer looked like the young scientist in search of a breakthrough research project.

His razor had missed a few bunches of hair and his teeth were stained from his two-pack-a-day habit. His glasses were halfway down his nose much of the time; he'd whip them off when a student asked him to review a slide. He'd stay huddled over the microscope until he'd answered every question. Then he'd pull his handkerchief from his hip pocket, wipe his glasses carefully and walk away.

Every year this man was voted the most admired teacher. It was the course in Human Genetics that stirred the imagination of some of our class. Gregor Mendel's studies years before had set the stage for some insight into heredity. We learned about chromosomes and genes. We were taught that there were 48 chromosomes in the genetics class. It wasn't until 1956 that this "fact" was changed. Now humans come into the world with 46 chromosomes, two of which are sex-determining chromosomes. Males have 44 numbered chromosomes and an X and a Y; females carry 44 chromosomes plus two XX chromosomes.

In quick sequence other discoveries changed the textbooks. Some people were discovered to have an extra chromosome; others had less than the normal complement. Down syndrome was found to have 47 chromosomes with the extra one at number 21, making the condition into what is known as trisomy. Armed with this ability to plot the chromosomes, we learned the cause of many handicapping states.

The Nobel prize in medicine was awarded for the discovery of the double helix structure of DNA and RNA. These terms became part of our vocabulary. How quickly had science progressed.

Adele was born before this enlightened era. She was one of a family of three boys and three girls. She was much tinier than her siblings but appeared sound in all other ways.

It was not until she was eleven years old that her family looked for medical attention. She was the smallest by far in her fifth grade class but her parents kept reminding themselves that there was a growth spurt just around the corner. The others had shot up at adolescence; they remembered trousers had to be let out; skirt hems had to be lengthened; shoe sizes grew bigger. None of these wonderful events occurred for Adele.

She was a lovely looking girl. Her skin was smooth without any hint of acne. Her features were delicate with a turned-up nose and her long blonde hair moved lazily when she shook her head. Adele loved to dance and she spent hours with her friends, practicing the latest steps. She knew the lyrics to all of the popular songs and could be found in the balcony of the neighborhood theater every Saturday, munching on popcorn and memorizing the love scenes of some Hollywood releases.

She collected posters of the movie stars and filled her bedroom walls with pictures of Garbo and Gable and Jimmy Stewart and Katherine Hepburn. The only dark cloud in her busy life was her growth delay. She wanted to be like the movie queens with their willowy figures and wear designer gowns and hold a cigarette holder in her hand or sip a cocktail in a Manhattan nightclub.

Her mirror revealed her boyish figure. There was no sign of breast buds; no change in body contour, not even the need to use antiperspirant cream or shave the hair on her legs. She was stuck at four feet eight inches and eighty-five pounds.

All of those genetic discoveries unlocked the secret of her child-like size but did nothing else. Adele faced a future where cuteness would be the most effective weapon she had. She would always be the pet of the group and could try to share their life style or she could retreat into semi-isolation.

We elected to put this new science to work. The answer came back quickly. Adele had Turner's syndrome. She had 45 chromosomes—not 46. The pattern was 45XO. She lacked the second chromosome and did not possess all of the characteristics of the average female as a result.

The findings were discussed with Adele and her parents. They had to be informed that her further growth would be minimal but hormone replacement would assure her that she would acquire a normal body build and could have symbolic menstruation even though she had no ovarian function of her own.

The information was shocking to Adele and her parents. They urged me to refer her to the appropriate specialist and begin therapy. Her spirits did not remain down very long and she soon became active in the drama club, chorus, sports, and found a job babysitting as well.

The estrogens worked beautifully—even to the point of producing some teenage pimples. She bounced into my office some years later. She was excited about her college plans. Her interest in the theater had shaped her choice of a career. As an aside, she mentioned that her boy-friend was enrolled in the same program.

I received a note of her marriage some time afterwards. The couple planned to live in Hawaii and teach at the high school level.

The animated girl with the 45XO count had thumbed her nose at nature. She sent me a long letter and a photograph of her family after they had been in Hawaii. Her husband was fully aware of her syndrome and they had adopted a baby. She might be barren, she wrote, in the biblical way, but that was not going to stop her. The baby was a hand-some boy, she said, twenty-one inches long at birth and she guaranteed me that he would be taller than her by the time he was ten years old.

CHAPTER 20

❧

Where Have All the Big Families Gone?

The two-year-old girl sitting on my lap let out a little cry. She stiffened as the camera's flash illuminated the room. I felt a warm flow dampen my trousers and realized that fear can defeat toilet training. The family was proud that Susan never wet during the day and sometimes slept through the night in perfect control. Just not this time.

Three generations had congregated in the empty waiting room of my office. I had phoned Hannah, the grandmother of all those children and told her that the newspaper's photographer wanted a group picture of some of my patients. It was needed for a soon-to-be-featured article about physicians who had been in practice for fifty years or more.

There they were. Thirty-six grandchildren and counting. They were dressed as if they were going to church. The boys with jackets, slacks and ties; the girls with party dresses. All were squeaky clean. No long hair, no tattoos, no tongue or belly rings. What a sight they made, each child more attractive than the next, from the toddlers to the teenagers. One family who filled my waiting room, ready to pose for pictures and ready to follow the photographer's directions.

He took some shots of the group as they sat in a row; some when they were standing stiffly at attention and my favorite pose—all of those children making faces at the camera, sticking out their tongues at the photographer's request and acting like trained monkeys for a few minutes until they were told the "shoot" was finished. Then they headed for the cookies and soft drinks and were ready to head for home.

There weren't many families like theirs anymore. Most of my practice was made up of small numbers. Many had only one child or at the most two or three. Working mothers were the norm rather than the exception. They had to help provide the basic necessities, particularly if it was a single-parent home. It was difficult to work eight hours a day and find the energy to handle domestic duties as well.

Hannah was different. She was a homemaker. Her large brood occupied all of her time. Her husband's job was secure at the telephone company. He was one of the union's leaders and his salary and benefits took care of all of the family's needs. Hannah and Ted resisted the trend to have both parents find employment. They didn't long for two cars, a boat, a summer cottage and trips to Disneyland.

Hannah and Ted may have been throwbacks to an earlier generation but they didn't seem to mind. Hannah had a zest for life. She managed to turn menial tasks into enjoyable exercises. She had songs for doing the laundry, others for ironing. She'd turn on the radio and add her voice to a rendition of some golden oldie or imitate a diva at the Metropolitan Opera, gestures and all. And she had been known to dance a jig or two.

This family represented the ideal pediatric practice. They were with me from the beginning and I was a witness to the many medical event that shaped their lives. As I watched them file out of the office and waited for the photographer to pack up his equipment, several scenes came to mind.

Five decades of caring for Hannah and Ted's children flew by rapidly. The Second World War had ended and I had been discharged from the Navy and was anxious to begin practice in my home town. I had been away for a number of years and had lost touch with the medical establishment and didn't realize that it took time to become established. I wanted to be a solo doctor and thought that patients would flock to my door. It turned out that Ted and Hannah were among the only ones with daring enough to join my practice. I don't know how they decided to call my office, possibly the older doctors were too busy to accept new patients. Fortunately, we seemed to hit it off and our longterm doctor/patient relationship flourished. It helped that Ted had been in the service and was willing to trust his young family's care to a fellow veteran.

As the years went by and they had more children, we went through some trying times together. One terrible event nearly cost the lives of the entire family. A new heating unit had been installed in their family room and something malfunctioned. In minutes a fire started and spread rapidly through the house. Everyone escaped but two of the children suffered extensive burns and needed hospitalization and plastic surgery later on.

There were lesser accidents as well, ranging from dog bites to fractures and the usual contagious diseases. Measles, mumps, chickenpox made an appearance before the preventive vaccines were available. There were so many calls to their house in the early years of our medical partnership that it seemed my car was on automatic pilot much of the time.

A few unusual experiences came to mind. They were among the worries that we shared together.

The whole city was in the middle of a mini-epidemic. It was a peculiar kind of respiratory illness. It came on suddenly and was characterized by chills, fever and a stubborn cough. The adults complained of aching of their muscles and joints and had splitting headaches. The children behaved differently. They were irritable and hard to console. Some had high fevers with vomiting and diarrhea. Others had croup. They were hoarse and had increasing difficulty in getting air. It was frightening for parent and child but most often cool steam inhalations and watchful waiting were followed by full recovery.

Irene, Hannah's oldest daughter, called me during one of these outbreaks and asked me to prescribe medicine over the phone. She said that she knew it was "what's going around" and didn't want to waste my time with an office visit.

Doctors have learned that mistakes can be made by telephone diagnosis and treatment. I urged her to bring her daughter to the office for safety's sake.

She was hesitant. "John's got to be out on line repair by noon. The storm has messed everything up. Phones are out for lots of people. I can't drive myself. You know I'm due to deliver any day now."

"I'll see to it that you won't have to wait," I said. "You'll be back home within an hour. I promise."

They were prompt. Alice was quieter than usual. She didn't resist my examination at all. Her cheeks were flushed; her pulse was rapid; she had a little hoarseness . . . not much else. She didn't quarrel when I asked her to open her mouth and say, "Ah." Didn't have to use the dreaded tongue blade.

Her throat was a bit red and her nose was stuffy. There wasn't anything I could culture. It probably was that familiar "what's going around" that Irene talked about. In all my years in practice, I'd never been able to make that diagnosis scientifically and yet everyone knew what it was and were satisfied with the label.

The only misgiving I had was Alice's docile behavior; so out of character for her. She had even accepted a Barbie sticker instead of throwing it on the floor in her usual defiance.

I told Irene to take her home, force fluids and give her some acetaminophen for fever. If she showed any change she was to give me a ring right away.

She was relieved and called John from his spot in the waiting room. He picked Alice up and carried her to the car while Alice followed slowly behind.

The rest of my morning was uneventful. I was in our small office kitchen starting my lunch break when my secretary buzzed me.

"Alice's mother wants to talk to you," she said. "Guess her daughter's worse and her husband's left for work. She's scared. Will you pick up on line #2?

Irene was sobbing. "She's so much worse, doctor. I'm all alone with her now and I don't know what to do." She went on. "I can't reach John now. He's out there someplace. The storm, you know, has all the crews out helping." A pause and then. "She's not able to swallow a thing. I gave her a warm drink as you suggested. She couldn't get any of it down. Poor baby—can't even swallow her own saliva."

I cut in. "No neighbors around to help you? Things certainly have changed in a couple of hours. Don't have her lie down in bed, keep her sitting up and I'll be out as soon as I can."

How much easier it would have been with today's support system. But this was Pediatrics in 1958. There was no 911 service nor ready access to ambulances. Doctors saw sick children in their offices or at home. Emergency rooms were in their infancy and were not the first facility in times of trouble as they are today.

It was about a six-mile drive to their home. The snow plows had cleared the main roads but the side streets were hard to negotiate. The snow was piled in high drifts and the driveway to my patient's home was waist-high and impassable by car. John probably had parked on the street last night or so.

Irene was waiting at the front door, motioning me to hurry. I carried my medical bag in front of me and entered their house. One look at Alice and the diagnosis was apparent. She had epiglottitis and it had moved along rapidly, threatening to shut off her breathing.

I raced to the telephone . . . theirs was still working . . . and called the pediatric floor. The resident promised he would have everything in place when my patient reached the hospital.

Irene bundled Alice up and asked me to hold her while she put on her own coat and boots and we headed for my car.

Alice was fighting for air. She made croaking sounds with each deep breath and her chest wall retracted with deep indentations.

Irene sat in the front seat with Alice on what remained of her lap. We started toward the hospital. I looked over at Alice. She was barely awake but I could see that she was still breathing. Deep painful breaths interspersed with an occasional cry as she tried to swallow the accumulated secretions in her throat.

I considered the various alternatives. My bag was within easy reach. If her breathing became even more labored, I could pull over to the side of the road and attempt to do a tracheotomy without anesthesia. Irene would have to hold her daughter down while I made an incision in her windpipe. What would I use to keep the tracheal incision open? There was nothing in my bag that could function properly. Maybe the cap of my fountain pen would do.

There had to be a better choice. We had left the cluster of homes in Irene and John's development and were on the main highway en route to the hospital. Traffic was rather heavy and there were traffic lights every few blocks. I had to get a police escort or I might lose Alice.

"Irene, hold her tight," I said. "I'm going to speed up . . . go through red lights if necessary and get to the hospital as fast as I can. Maybe a prowl car will stop us and when they see you and Alice, we'll have their help."

She nodded. I honked the horn, swerved around car after car. The trip was made in record time but I did not attract the police's attention despite the flagrant violation of the law.

The ENT doctor was waiting for us at the hospital. He took one look at Alice and hustled her up to the operating suite.

Irene signed all the consent forms for surgery and went to the parents' room to wait. She didn't want to be alone and called her mother and asked her to be with her while Alice was in the operating room.

Hannah had been expecting a maternity call, not an emergency for Alice. She hurried to be with Irene. As she hustled toward the hospital, a police siren made her pullover to the side of the road. She put the ticket in her purse and joined Irene in the vigil.

Kurt was Ted and Hannah's oldest grandchild. There is something magical about the birth of the first grandchild on either side of the family.

I remember the excitement when he arrived. That initial newborn examination was witnessed by a large viewing audience. They had lined up in the hall and were peering through the window of the nursery as I inspected Kurt. They watched as the baby withstood the head-to-toe examination; checking to make sure that everything was in working order. When I indicated that he had passed with flying colors, they gestured that I should hold him up so that they could record this important event on film.

Other births followed, of course, and in time there were thirty-six grandchildren with more on the way.

Kurt, being the first, may have been his grandfather's favorite. Although he would deny it vehemently, Ted had more time to enjoy the various stages of infancy and childhood, now that he was semi-retired, and did seem to concentrate on Kurt.

He told everyone who would listen that this young child was quite special. Not that he was bragging, he would say, "but just look at the shoulders on this kid. He's got the build of an Olympic athlete already."

In truth, Kurt was remarkably well coordinated. He walked before he was nine months old, climbed onto counters and opened cabinet doors before he cut his molars. He was able to ride a two-wheeled bicycle by the age of three and he learned to swim and roller skate before he started kindergarten.

His doting grandfather taught him to play catch and how to bat and even coached his soccer team when Kurt was seven. Every sport was appealing to Kurt but football and basketball captured most of his attention. He played on all the school teams in early high school and was considered to be a natural by all of the coaches at each level of competition, and they weren't biased like his grandfather.

When Kurt had his sports physical before his junior year in high school, he was in the best shape of his career. He had spent the entire summer working at a construction site. It was demanding physically but he enjoyed the chance to stay in shape for football and to earn money toward his car insurance.

He weighed in at two hundred ten pounds and was six-foot-three-inches tall. His body was firm and his muscles were well outlined. The weight training program once school started would add bulk to his frame and increase his stamina as well.

His hair was longer than his father liked and was nearly platinum from the long hours under the sun. I noticed that there were more freckles than before and that there was even a fair start on a mustache. This latter feature would have to go when football season began and his hair would need to be shorn to comply with the coach's rules.

Kurt looked like a Viking warrior and this resemblance was not lost on the cheerleaders at his school. They did their best to get his attention and prayed that he might notice them.

When I finished my examination he pocketed the completed form and left the office. He had no complaints and had no questions other than soliciting my opinion on the use of various performance-enhancing substances. He seemed to agree that there was no need for additional vitamins or protein drinks and offered negative comment about the role of anabolic steroids.

Kurt had started most of the games during the last season as a tight end and was counted on to be an All Star. He lived up to all the expectations and his team won the sectional championship. A number of scouts from the major universities sat in the stands during the playoff series and Kurt was the target of most of their interests. A scholarship was a certainty . . . his task would be to decide what program had the best academic and athletic qualities.

When the season ended, Kurt called my office. He asked if I could see him that week. He had a few concerns and wanted to talk.

I was taken aback when he sat across the desk from me. It had been six or seven months since his sports physical and he had lost that healthy glow. His face was drawn and he seemed to be tired, so out of character for this usually robust young man.

"Doctor, I can't put my finger on what's wrong," he began. "I'm getting plenty of rest but I'm exhausted most of the time. And of all things, my appetite is way off. You know my reputation, I eat everything in sight."

"How long have you been feeling this way?" I asked.

"It started just before the season ended. I'd never felt this way before. I thought I'd be o.k. when all the games were finished, but I'm just dragging all the time."

"Have you had any other symptoms?" I wanted to know. "Shortness of breath, chest pain, headache, sick to your stomach?"

"None of those," he said. "Except for the appetite being down . . . oh, I have had some cramps in my gut lately. Forgot about that."

He stepped on the scale and we saw that he had lost twenty pounds since his sport physical. The full-scale exam was not alarming otherwise. He did have some abdominal tenderness, but no masses could be felt. He wasn't jaundiced but was slightly pallid.

We drew some blood and sent if off to the laboratory. His urine sample was negative and we did a tuberculin test also. I wanted him to come back in one week and we'd discuss his lab tests and re-examine him.

Kurt was concerned enough to have his father come with him for moral support at the re-appointment.

He had some new symptoms to report. His abdominal cramps had become more severe and he had some loose, mucusy stools with traces of blood. He told me that he had been feeling chilly and that he had been running a slight fever.

The diagnosis was becoming clearer. His abdominal discomfort and the laboratory tests were suggestive of an inflammatory bowel disease.

Kurt and his father heard the news and were stunned. They knew that this type of illness was difficult to manage and meant a major change in his life.

"Crohn's disease," said his father. "You think that's what Kurt might have? My God, isn't that what President Eisenhower had? Kurt's only seventeen. Can somebody his age have it?"

"It's quite common in young people," I said. "We've got to prove it first with some x-rays and endoscopic exams. Then we can begin to treat him and get a handle on his condition.

The endoscopy and barium studies confirmed our clinical impression. Kurt was started on an aggressive treatment course. It was hard for him to accept his illness. It meant that there would be a radical change in his life and his plans for sports and college had to be put on hold.

His days were spent trying to regain his lost weight and energy. The medication was helpful but there were side effects from the collection of drugs necessary to control his illness.

Spring sports were out. He had an unexpected setback after several months of treatment and had to be hospitalized. He had developed severe abdominal cramps and during one of his visits to the specialist, a mass was discovered in his pelvis.

A large abscess was found at the time of an exploratory operation. A twenty-inch segment of his intestine had to be removed and he needed total parenteral nutrition to allow the inflammatory reaction to resolve.

After a two-week stay in the hospital he was able to return to school. He did well on his exams and was ready to start his senior year. The future did not appear as promising as before. The many offers for athletic scholarships disappeared. He knew that any scholarship would be academic, not athletic.

Kurt's summer vacation was spent on the practice field of a city park near his home. He spent hours with one of his teammates. His return as a tight end was impossible. He had been told that contact sports were taboo.

His role would be very different and of a minor nature. Not much glory as a place kicker, the position he would try to fill, would not be very glamorous, but if he could make the team, even in that limited way, he would be satisfied.

It was an odd feeling to find a seat on the bench as his teammates trotted on the field for the opening game. They had honored Kurt by selecting him as a co-captain. He had two chances to compete when the team scored touchdowns and both points after attempts were successful.

The season went along; his team won all but one game and again went in the playoffs as defending champions.

His family watched as a Kurt-less offense and their opponents battled to a 7-7 tie with less than a minute to play.

In a script that could have been written in Hollywood, his team had possession of the ball and drove to the twenty-five yard line.

Kurt jogged onto the field. The ball was placed down and he waited for the snap from center. The ball was held in place. He watched it as it sailed through the uprights.

His role was less dominating than in last year's victory, but this time when he was lifted onto his teammates shoulders, it was much sweeter.

CHAPTER 21

༄

Nowhere to Turn

Sid, the mailman, rang the doorbell one day. "Here's a package you'll have to sign for, Doc. Probably more books."

He placed the large carton on my desk, waited to collect my signature, and sighed as he headed toward the door.

"You guys have to study all the time, don't you? Look at all the stuff in your bookcases already. Do you ever have the time to read what you've got?"

"Sid, much of it is out of date. I try to read whenever I can. But it's not possible to do more than scratch the surface. To tell you the truth, I have a problem. I can't throw a book away. It seems like a sin. Somebody tried to put what he knew down on paper and I think it would be wrong to chuck it in the wastebasket."

"Yeah, I see what you mean. But I've got some news for you. We're going to have another baby. Zelda found out just last week. How about that?"

I gripped his hand. "Sid, that's terrific. You must be thrilled. Great news."

He went on. "We didn't think we'd have any more. After all, Louis will be fifteen in March and Zelda had all those miscarriages a couple of years ago. We had given up when this happened."

I followed him to the door. It was drizzling outside and there was a nasty wind that whipped through the empty lot next to my house. He made a dash toward his car and headed back to the post office.

Sid was a small, wiry man. He had closely cropped, reddish-brown hair with a few fine wires of grey and a suspicious thin spot on top. His movements were quick and he drummed his fingers together when he talked as if he were applauding his own cleverness. His voice was a rich baritone and his words were measured. Someone said that he sang in the choir and some chorale groups. He had been leaving the mail at my home for a dozen or more years and my children were sure that he read all of the postcards, particularly the ones sent from college with their final grades.

Our house was near the end of his route so he often would linger a few extra moments before heading home. We thought Sid was over-qualified for his job. He could talk about any subject, from baseball to opera, and was ready to debate political science or economics. He seemed out of place carrying a pouch of letters through the changing seasons rather than delivering a lecture on some college campus. But he didn't seem to resent his civil service job. Maybe he had abandoned all thoughts of returning to school and getting a degree. The regular paycheck gave him security and provided the basics for his family. Al-though he still talked wistfully about going back once he put aside a few thousand dollars, when Bobby was born he never mentioned his own career again.

Whenever Sid caught me at home on my day off, his conversation centered around his family. The birth of his son, Bobby, had changed his life. The baby's multiple congenital defects and the need for re-peated hospital admissions had exhausted the family's savings. Sid had a good insurance policy through his work but the expenses for travel and living accommodations away from home were overwhelming. Most of the time Zelda traveled with Bobby while Sid stayed home with Louis. He was able to earn much-needed extra income by moon-lighting at a hardware store at a nearby shopping mall.

Bobby had a rare condition known as arthrogryposis. He had con-tractures of all of his joints and casts were needed to correct the club-foot deformity that was present and several surgical admissions to re-lease his tight heel tendons. The curvature of the spine, scoliosis, would be deferred for a later date. It was certain that the family would face many years of medical care before Bobby would be able to have the semblance of a normal life.

Sid confided in me one day that he was concerned about his older son, Louis. Louis was starting his junior year in high school and had been affected by his parents precarious financial state. For years Sid had encouraged him to take all of the college preparatory courses and try to excel in his studies. The road to success later in life, Sid empha-sized, depended on higher education. He did not want Louis to have to settle for a dead-end job, but rather have a profession of his choice.

Louis had many interests ranging from business to law and politics. His grades were in the upper five percent of his class and he was involved in a variety of extracurricular activities as well. The interval between his junior and senior year brought still more stress into the life of his family. Zelda discovered a lump in her breast and it meant another chink in the family's health armor. The lesion was benign, fortunately, but Zelda was obsessed with the fear that something might happen to her or to Sid and was terrified that her two sons would be helpless without them.

Louis made an appointment with the guidance counselor when school began, thinking that his parents might need him to help as best he could with a part-time job because his father's budget would be unable to finance a junior college, let alone a private university.

His counselor promised to explore scholarship with opportunities but told him that he might wisely stay out of school for a year and set aside enough money for the first year's tuition. Most of the State's academic scholarships, he reminded Louis, only covered a small portion of the total cost.

Louis realized it was no one's fault. His parents wanted their children to achieve their dreams but his had to be delayed. He managed to find a part-time job at one of the factories, as an unskilled laborer. The pay was minimal and he could put no more than twelve hours of work at the factory and still go to school.

He began to complain of headaches and swallowed pill after pill in order to make it to school and work. There wasn't much time for recreation and there was little outlet for his pent-up anxieties. On one occasion he visited my office and poured out some of his concerns.

He had an air of hopelessness that worried me. He thought that he was doomed to failure despite his brilliant school record. He felt a deep sadness and had little hope that his life had value. He thought of himself as an insignificant part of the family who would never be able to live up to his parents hopes for his future. Louis felt incapable of succeeding on his own.

He was the characteristic patient with adolescent depression. This condition had been receiving increasing attention in the medical literature. At a critical time in their teen years, some young people become unreachable. They are without joy; all flavor leaves their lives; in its place is a pessimism that is difficult to treat.

It was past my skills to help him emerge from his distorted view of his life. He needed psychiatric attention but there was little likelihood that he would consent to have another doctor see him nor could he afford the long therapy sessions.

Louis promised me he would follow some of the suggestions I had made and assured me that he would seek counseling if he didn't feel better.

At the end of the school year there was an opening for full-time employment at the factory. Louis felt that he might be able to conquer some of his doubts if he had regular hours and a decent weekly salary.

He went to work as part of the crew in the bottling department. It was monotonous and repetitious . . . the sameness of every day's duties lulled him into an automatic management of his machine. He paid little attention to the safety rules for the equipment and while daydreaming one morning, his sleeve became entangled and his arm was drawn into the machine.

He felt tremendous pain and yelled for help. By the time the foreman ran to him and turned off the switch, his arm was mangled and useless. The injury was so severe with damage to muscle, bone, nerve, and blood supply that nothing could be done to preserve full function of his arm. He was told that the surgeons had considered amputation but felt that although his limb was useless it would be less of a blow to accept the deformity than to have an empty sleeve.

It was a difficult time for an already-troubled young man. He was unable to return to work and refused to go back to school. He spent most of his days in his room listening to music or sleeping. He became preoccupied with thoughts of death and wondered if he could find the courage to take his own life.

Sid and Zelda were very supportive of their son but knew that the healing process and the emotional consequences of his injury would require many months before he would be ready to talk about the future.

They had an appointment for Bobby in Philadelphia for the next round of orthopedic surgery. Louis assured them that he was willing to stay home alone and said he would call them if he needed anything. Sid was torn between the worries about each of his sons but promised they would check with him by phone daily.

The day after Sid, Zelda and Bobby left, Louis searched the medicine cabinet in his parents' bedroom, looking for pain pills or tranquilizers. If he took enough of them, he might be able to drift into eternity and end his troubles. All he could find were antacids for Sid's stomach disorder and some of his mother's estrogen tablets.

He wrote a long note telling his parents how much he loved them and how he would miss his brother. He pinned the note to his pillow and ran out of the house.

Their next door neighbor's car was unlocked. Louis looked around and saw no one in sight. He had a little difficulty with only one good arm, but he managed to hot-wire the car and headed towards the freeway.

His mind was made up. He pressed down on the accelerator and raced down the expressway. He passed car after car and ignored the loud sound of the police siren some distance behind him. His hands were sweaty and he felt flushed. He looked in the rear-view mirror and saw the squad car drawing nearer. He had never driven alone before and wondered how he could slow down gradually and swerve the car off the highway.

He pumped the brakes lightly, rounded a curve with the police in hot pursuit. He saw a sign for a rest stop and headed for the turnoff. His speed slowed and he crashed into the brick wall of the reception center.

The air bag imploded and his journey was over. Louis offered no resistance when the officers pulled him from the wreckage. He was dazed but coherent. There were no apparent injuries and he was able to answer all of their questions.

He hadn't been drinking, he said, and he was not on drugs. They could run all the tests they wanted. He didn't care. No, he didn't have a license and he knew he was speeding. Yes, his head hurt from the impact and he thought he might throw up. Could they let him go over to the side of the road and make sure he wasn't going to mess up their car and his clothes?

The police called a tow truck and the ambulance, even though he protested that he didn't need to be checked for injuries. The doctors in the emergency room looked him over and sent him for x-rays of his head and cervical spine. He was kept overnight for observation even though the x-rays were negative and his symptoms had abated.

The doctors called Sid in Philadelphia and told him about Louis' accident. He wanted to make sure his son was not seriously injured and was comforted when he heard Louis' voice. Zelda would stay with Bobby and he would be with him in six or seven hours.

Sid said nothing when he entered Louis' room. He glanced at his son and then walked slowly to his side. He hugged his six-foot teenager and sobbed as he saw the vacant look in his eyes. How could this have happened? Should I have seen it coming?

They collected Louis' belongings and waited for the police representative to appear. Sid was handed a form and told that Louis was to make a court appearance in ten days.

My neighborhood had a number of professional people living along Sid's route. He had heard that George Hampton was a top-notch lawyer. He had seen him occasionally when he was making his deliveries and hoped that he might be willing to help his son during this crisis.

He called George Hampton's office and his secretary said that he wasn't taking any new cases, but she agreed to tell him that his mail carrier wanted to ask him a few questions. Hampton was out of the office, she said, but was expected back in an hour or so.

"Sid," the voice said, "my secretary told you that I wasn't taking any new cases. That's true. But you've been leaving mail at my house for a long time, maybe I can make an exception in your case. I'd like to help you out if I can."

They arranged for a meeting at the lawyer's office for the following day. Sid and Louis sat nervously in the waiting room, waiting to be called.

George Hampton saw a tall, frightened-looking young man sitting near his father, staring straight ahead. He nodded to Sid and turned toward Louis and said. "Bring me up to speed, will you? What happened? You borrowed a car, lost control . . . is that it?"

He studied Louis carefully. It was not unusual for a sixteen-year-old do something as stupid as he did, but this young man didn't seem like the others. He didn't have a defiant air. He seemed lost, out of contact—he wasn't dressed like most of the other kids. Clean shirt and sweat shirt, jeans that fit—he stopped his mental inventory and said, "The charges against you are serious. We may be able to do something about them since you are a youthful offender." He paused and asked, "But what happened to your arm?"

The lawyer's eyes were focused on Louis' left arm, which dangled by his side. Had he had polio or was it a birth defect?

Louis said quietly, "I had an accident at work last summer. Got it caught in a machine."

"My God, young man, can you manage all right? I mean, can you get by with one good arm? I don't want to pry, but it must be hard to drive a car or operate a machine."

The lawyer listened as Louis described the accident. He jotted down a few notes and said, "I'll get back to you in a couple days. I had a case like yours with a similar machine five or six years ago. Wonder if it's the same design. Could be the manufacturer's fault, not yours."

George Hampton was able to have Louis' records kept clear and he was placed under the court's supervision for the next year. There were definite parallels to the injury case that Hampton had mentioned. Many phone calls, hours in the law library and finally a settlement of six figures for Louis.

At my insistence the young man found help with a psychiatrist at the medical center. His depression took many sessions before there was improvement. Finally, he completed his last year of high school and I lost track of him. Sid mentioned every now and then that Louis was going away to college.

Some years later I had a phone call from one of my sons. He was in his first year at law school and found the going tough. Lots and lots of reading, he said. "Say, Dad," he added, "there's a fellow in my class. Nice guy. He said you used to take care of him when he was young. His name is Louis Thompson. You might remember him. He's got a bad arm, but it doesn't seem to hold him back. We've been studying together."

My son was right. It didn't hold him back at all. Louis Thompson finished law school and began practice in our community. Later he was selected as an assistant to the Attorney General dealing with Consumer Affairs and Negligence cases, and is still serving in that capacity.

CHAPTER 22

⤚

Father Gabriel

My wife and I sat in the back row of the cathedral. The ceremony was overpowering. The enraptured look on all the faces made this ordination unforgettable. It was not my religion, not my house of worship, but it was easy to be carried away by the service.

The young man stood before the congregation at this time of sanctification, ready to assume his priesthood. He was about to fulfill a pledge made many years before—in a hospital room, with a much different audience observing him.

At that time his mother and father were at his side, waiting for him to awaken from a prolonged coma. He was in a short hospital gown, with ties in the back, nearly hidden under the oxygen canopy. His arms were immobile at his sides. The steady drip, drip of IV glucose carried energy throughout his body.

For twenty days I had observed the same scene. An unconscious youth in a state of hibernation; no clue that he would ever emerge. His parents were part of the scenery of the bleak room. When I made my daily rounds, they'd search for a sign that he had improved; failing to sense a change, they'd return to keep their vigil.

He had never convulsed before this illness. They had heard a cry and then a crash as he hit the hardwood floor. Jerky movements of his arms, tightly clenched jaws, heavy breathing and deep stupor, as if all connection to the world had been cut, the master switch turned off. When I reached their home, he was no longer having fits. He did not respond to any stimuli, painful or otherwise. Then he began to twitch again, a series of violent muscle contractions involving his whole body. They could not be controlled with the medications in my bag, and it took large amounts of barbiturates in the emergency room before the agitations ended.

We ran test after test on his spinal fluid and his blood and sent specimens to the State Research Laboratory before the diagnosis of equine encephalitis could be proven. We theorized that he must have been bitten by a mosquito carrying the virus while he was playing in the marshy fields near his home. That was the diagnosis I presented to the parents, but I couldn't provide any treatment. There was no effective therapy for this nervous system infection. We could just maintain some level of nutrition either by tube or vein, and sedate him so he wouldn't convulse again, and wait.

We called in some infectious disease experts who tapped his knees, looked at his pupils, studied the brain waves and turned away when they acknowledged it was encephalitis. They reiterated the uncertain prognosis for the young patient.

"Have you given up too, Doctor?" his father asked me as the weeks passed. "I haven't given up," I said. "It's just that I realize nothing's changing. He doesn't react. He's the way he was the day he took sick."

"Everything hasn't been tried," the man said quietly. "We haven't given prayer a chance. It's not hopeless, you know. We have faith and we know he's going to get better."

"I'd be the last one to argue against that."

Miracles aren't always instantaneous. But a flicker of an eyelid one day; then a movement of his hand. A process of rebirth almost. A groan of distress was greeted as if the veil was being lifted, and he was reaching out to the world again. Inch by inch he left his hibernation. The pace of recovery accelerated. He was able to sit and feed himself, to talk and at least take a few wobbly steps down the hall.

I began to discuss rehabilitation and arranged for the next weeks to be spent at home. A physiotherapist was engaged to stop by and help him exercise his weakened muscles.

He was in a wheelchair the day he went home. His father turned to me as his son left the hospital room.

"Doctor, you're invited to his ordination." There was a huge smile on his face. He piled the mass of cards from his son's classmates into a suitcase and placed them on the boy's lap. "It'll be a few years, of course, but we'll remind you when the time comes."

"Thanks a lot," I said. "Even though I don't know what you're talking about."

"I know you don't. When I said that we were going to pray he'd wake up and be himself again, we made a promise. He would give his life to serve, to be a priest. You'll see, it will happen."

I wouldn't question this decision though it was not made by the boy. The story of Abraham and Isaac was being replayed and faith was as strong as in biblical days.

They sent me an invitation, as they said they would. Their son, Father Gabriel, was to be ordained.

CHAPTER 23

✎

From Babel to Symphony

The household was in chaos. There were half-empty bottles of formula and a pacifier on the bedroom dresser. Packages of disposable diapers were near the new baby's crib and a playpen filled with toys was in the corner of the room with a crying two-and-a-half-year-old waiting to be picked up.

The newborn had been with them for nearly two weeks. They couldn't resist adding her to their life. Cindy was a beautiful black child from the inner city. Her fifteen-year-old mother had neither the desire nor the means to care for the baby. There was no extended family willing to lend a hand and foster home care was the temporary solution until adoption could be arranged.

Dominick and Myrna were social workers who had been working with indigent girls for the last ten years. They were childless themselves and longed to enrich their lives with children. They said lots and lots of kids were what they wanted. The need was great, they felt, to offer some of these abandoned babies love and a stable home.

Their first adventure in parenthood was a five-year-old girl from Croatia. Her parents were killed during the Balkan conflict and she was brought to our community by a refugee support group and was placed with relatives. They felt that they couldn't care for another child and once she became a candidate for adoption, Myrna begged her supervisor to use her influence and arrange for a legal adoption.

The red tape was an annoying obstacle but Kathryn was theirs after an interminable wait. Both Myrna and Dominick were captivated by Kathryn. She was a quiet, withdrawn child who had been shuffled from one place to another after her parents died. It was difficult to communicate with her at first because of the language barrier but Myrna found that Kathryn learned quickly and after a few months in their home she was ready for kindergarten.

She was a delight; a child starved for love and finding two people eager to spend hours with her—reading stories, drawing pictures, singing and laughing and pushing away the memories of yesterday's struggles.

Dominick had grown up in a family of seven brothers. He was fascinated by this delicate little girl. Roughhousing was unthinkable, of course, and at first he was ill at ease. But when she laughed when he was silly and when she hugged him as he tucked her in bed, he melted, and was her slave forever.

Kathryn withstood the visits to my office and was braver than most when she was examined and her immunizations were brought up to date. I, too, was charmed by her sweetness and innocence. It was a relief to find a child uninfluenced by TV characters and unfamiliar with French fries and cheeseburgers.

They felt that they wanted more children and knew that Kathryn deserved to have a brother or sister. Dominick decided he could stretch the budget a bit more and assume the added responsibility.

Kathryn took to Mei Ling immediately. Mei Ling was an emaciated little child who had been in an orphanage in China when Myrna heard of her. She had been abandoned by her parents and was one of the many unwanted children cared for by the State.

It was hard to find a home for Mei Ling. She had been delivered by a midwife and had suffered a birth injury. Her left side was spastic and she was undernourished.

Myrna's heart went out to the helpless child. How could she and Dominick repair the damage done by poor obstetrical care, growth delay and a handicapping birth defect? There was no question that they would accept the challenge and try to bring Mei Ling out of the slavery of indifference into a warm and caring home.

Mei Ling needed more than love. One of my orthopedic colleagues had been in China several years earlier. He had worked in a clinic in one of the provinces where supplies were limited and equipment was antiquated. The Chinese physicians were talented and compassionate but their caseloads were enormous. Children like Mei Ling were on an endless waiting list and her turn had yet to come when Myrna received word that she would be coming to America.

My orthopedic friend started the first of many corrective procedures within a month of Mei Ling's arrival. Her dislocated hip required a hospital admission followed by a lengthy rehabilitation. Myrna used the long massage and exercise sessions to grow closer to the child. They passed the time during the monotonous workouts playing simple word games and Mei Ling grasped her new language quickly. She rarely spoke in her native tongue, only reserving it when she and Kathryn tried to tease each other. They'd frown and pretend they didn't understand what was being said, and then would laugh and rattle off sentences in English.

Myrna and Dominick discovered that the babel of the beginning years disappeared and that their growing family had developed strong bonds. Kathryn and Mei Ling mothered their little sister, Cindy, and included her in all of their activities.

Each of the children shared their parents love of music. Dominick, true to his heritage, was an opera buff with a complete repertoire, sung in Italian or German, while Myrna had dreamed of being a concert violinist before her career of social work and marriage intervened.

The family's entertainment was not passive. TV was seldom turned on and Disney videos and computer games were unknown in their household. Kathryn selected the piano as her instrument of choice; Mei Ling opted for violin lessons and enjoyed the chance to entertain the others with a duet with Myrna. Cindy loved the spotlight and held an imaginary microphone in her hand and sang whenever anyone would listen.

By the time Kathryn was twelve years old, Mei Ling nearly ten and Cindy almost eight, they were ready to perform at the church's family night. Three sisters, of different backgrounds had been blended into something special. I sat with Myrna and Dominick as their daughters gave their first "concert." The audience was generous with their applause and the girls curtsied and joined their parents and waited for the next act.

Although they would never be asked to appear at Carnegie Hall or even on the stage at a State Fair, I knew that these three lives had been saved by their parents' devotion.